T0274039

FABRIC STAMPING

A Simple Guide to Surface Design Using Block Printing and Foam Stamps

LORI WENGER

BETTER DAY BOOKS®

HAPPY · CREATIVE · CURATED

Easy Patterns Download!

Download all the ready-to-use patterns for the projects in this book at the following link. All these patterns are already included in the book, but if you need extras or simply don't want to remove pages, you can print the patterns at home!

www.betterdaybooks.com/fabric-stamping-patterns-download

Fabric Stamping © 2024 by Lori Wenger and Better Day Books, Inc.

Publisher: Peg Couch
Book Designer: Llara Pazdan
Cover Designer: Ashlee Wadeson
Editor: Colleen Dorsey
Photo Stylist: Lori Wenger
Photographer (projects): Jason Masters
Photographer (step-by-step): Lori Wenger

Library of Congress Control Number: 2023945553

ISBN: 978-0-7643-6800-4
Printed in China
10 9 8 7 6 5 4 3 2 1

Copublished by Better Day Books, Inc., and Schiffer Publishing, Ltd.

BETTER DAY BOOKS®

Better Day Books
P.O. Box 21462
York, PA 17402
Phone: 717-487-5523
Email: hello@betterdaybooks.com
www.betterdaybooks.com
@better_day_books

SCHIFFER
PUBLISHING

Schiffer Publishing
4880 Lower Valley Road
Atglen, PA 19310
Phone: 610-593-1777
Fax: 610-593-2002
Email: info@schifferbooks.com
www.schifferbooks.com

This title is available for promotional or commercial use, including special editions. Contact info@schifferbooks.com for more information.

This book is dedicated to my Grandma. Her creativity and skilled hands ignited a lifelong love of crafting in me! I love you, GG!

CONTENTS

WELCOME

Hello, and welcome to the world of fabric surface design! I'm so happy you picked up this book, and I'm honored to be part of your creative journey. Whether you're a lover of bold patterns and bright colors like me, or you simply find joy in making things, this book is for you.

Designing your own fabric is such a gratifying experience. In this book, we'll explore techniques that will inspire you to create your very own unique textiles.

For the first technique, we'll dive into the world of stamping, using stamps made from ordinary craft foam. These handmade stamps deliver a crisp, modern look.

Next, we'll learn about block printing. Block printing is an ancient art form with great significance for many cultures. This more traditional method for printing on fabric allows you to create extremely intricate designs.

In the final chapter, you'll find more tips, tricks, and inspiring ideas that will offer endless possibilities for creating one-of-a-kind textiles.

Throughout the book, we'll explore everything from home décor to wearable art to personalized gifts. The step-by-step photos and instructions, helpful hints, and inspiring projects will guide you through the process. So, grab your tools, let your creativity soar, and get ready to create your own works of art!

M LoriWenger

MEET THE AUTHOR

How did you first get into crafting? Have you always been creative?

I'm so grateful to have had parents who always encouraged my creativity. When I was a child, drawing was my absolute favorite pastime. I loved drawing people, designing clothes, and doodling patterns. As I grew older and was introduced to a wider array of tools, materials, and possibilities, my passion for all things "artsy" grew right along with me.

What drew you to fabric stamping? What do you love about it?

Occasionally, some of my dearest friends will request that I organize a crafting activity for us to do together. I'm always delighted! I always love the idea of creating something that is both beautiful and functional. In this instance, we decided to create tea towels that would complement our own kitchens. We had a great time sitting and working, all the while enjoying each other's company and conversation. The idea for this book took root there.

Fabric stamping is particularly fun for me because I've always been drawn to vibrant, vivid textiles. This stamping method has given me the chance to bring my own designs to life!

What do you love most about crafting?

I feel such a sense of accomplishment and joy when I'm making things with my hands. Often, I craft just for the sole purpose of creating. I find so much relaxation in it. It's like therapy to me!

What are your favorite things to craft?

Gifts! I love creating handmade, personalized gifts. It lets the receiver know you are really thinking about them. I like to incorporate thoughtfulness, shared memories, and uniqueness into gift giving. Cards, jewelry, tea towels, and photo albums are some of my favorite gifts to give. I also love receiving handmade gifts!

What is one of your favorite handmade gifts you've given?

Not long ago, my grandmother and I were sitting in her backyard, admiring her lovely, full hydrangeas. I snuck over and stole one flower from the bush. I preserved the flower inside a resin charm and attached it to a necklace. I gave it to her on her 90th birthday.

What do you struggle with as an artist?

Like many artists, perfectionism and self-doubt are ever-present hurdles when I'm working. In more-recent years, I've noticed I can become overwhelmed with constant stimulation. As technology evolves, the information and sensory input are both an inspiration and an obstacle. It can be difficult to sift through it all sometimes. When I'm feeling this way, I try to remind myself to put my phone down and find other sources of inspiration. Some of my favorites are going on a bike ride, visiting an art museum, listening to music, flea market shopping, and drawing.

What brings you joy in your free time?

I have a strong community of friends and family nearby, so quality time with the people I love is most precious to me. I also take great pleasure in supporting our local theaters, undertaking imaginative projects with my two kids, neighborhood walks with my husband, breathing new life into my 1960s home, and cozying up with my sweet dog, Ruby.

Do you listen to music/podcasts while you work?

Yes, I often get lost in podcasts and music while I create. I enjoy a wide spectrum of podcasts from educational and self-improvement to purely entertaining comedy and true-crime content. As for music, I gravitate toward a slower tempo and a storytelling element. Taylor Swift was on the regular rotation for a lot of this book.

What do you hope readers will get from this book?

This book is meant to inspire. My hope is that it will guide, motivate, and serve as a jumping-off point for your own personal journey of creativity.

What is your advice to a beginner?

Just get started; that's always the hardest part. Gather your materials, prepare your workspace, and dive in. The worst thing that can happen is that you'll mess up. And guess what—everyone does! Mistakes are just part of the process. They can often lead to an unexpected yet amazing result, and they can always help us grow!

Where can we learn more about you?

You can find me at www.michallorenart.com and on Instagram at both @michal_loren_art and @lori_wenger!

Lori Wenger is an author, illustrator, pattern designer, photo stylist, and lifelong creative from Arkansas. She is the author of many craft publications, including *Boho Jewelry*, *Aromatherapy Jewelry*, *Cool String Art*, *Simple Home Décor*, *Resin Jewelry*, and *Clay Jewelry*. Lori is also the founder of the Michal Loren design studio, where she creates color-filled illustrations that celebrate everyday joys of life. Learn more at www.michallorenart.com and @michal_loren_art on Instagram.

CHAPTER 1:
Getting Started

Are you ready to dive into fabric stamping? Take a few minutes to review this chapter if you've never stamped before (or even if you have)—it contains all the basic info about tools and supplies you'll need to have on hand and guidance about choosing colors.

Tools & Supplies

Each project includes its own specific supplies list. All the tools and supplies we're using in this book are beginner level, easy to use, available at your local craft store, and perfect for making the projects! For block printing, there are many great starter kits available.

Here is a list of general supplies to have on hand that are used throughout the book for various techniques:

- 8½" x 11" (22 x 28 cm) sheets of thin acrylic glass (found in the glass section of your local craft store)
- Prewashed, premade fabric products
- Acrylic craft paint
- Textile medium (also known as fabric paint medium or fabric medium)
- Fabric block-printing ink
- Craft foam with adhesive backing
- Soft rubber or linoleum carving blocks
- Carving tools
- Soft rubber brayer
- Baren (optional)
- Paint palette
- 1" (2.5 cm) craft foam brushes

- ½" (1.3 cm) and ¼" (0.6 cm) sponge daubers
- Small paintbrush
- Pencil
- Tracing paper
- Cutting mat
- Craft knife
- Permanent marker
- Ruler/straightedge
- Parchment paper
- Wet wipes or wet paper towels
- Double-sided tape
- Blue painter's tape
- Tweezers

Turn the page to learn more about a few of the more specialized items that you may not be familiar with.

TEXTILE MEDIUM: Textile medium, also known as fabric medium, is a product you'll use a lot in this book. You mix it with acrylic paint, then apply the mixed paint to fabric. This allows the fabric to remain soft and flexible and to keep its original texture. Without it, the fabric will become stiff and crunchy where the paint was applied. Textile medium also helps the paint bond to the fabric, preventing flaking and making the piece washable.

ACRYLIC PAINT: For many of the projects in this book, you'll use traditional acrylic craft paint. I love it because it comes in a ton of colors, it's affordable, it dries quickly, and it cleans up with ease. And, when mixed with textile medium, craft paint adheres nicely to fabric.

PAINT PALETTE: For just about every project in this book, you'll need a paint palette of some sort. This could be anything from a purchased palette (with separate wells, like the one shown in the photos throughout the book) to a paper plate, a plastic lid, or even small cups or jars. If you're using a single flat surface, make sure you have plenty of space so that your paint colors don't run together. If you won't be able to finish your project in one sitting, use an airtight container to seal your paint so you can leave and come back to it later.

FABRIC INK: You should use fabric block-printing ink for all the block-printing projects in this book. These inks are specially formulated for the application and typically have a thick consistency that makes them ideal for rolling out. I used Speedball's Fabric Block Printing Ink for all the block-printing projects in this book. Keep in mind that the ink begins to dry out quickly, so when it's time to work with ink, you'll want to have everything laid out and ready so you can work fast. When stamping a large surface, like the table runner project, you might need to store your mixed ink in an airtight container. However, once it has been stamped on fabric, it takes a long time to fully dry—about 36 hours. Allow it to cure for a week before use

or laundering. I will show you how to mix the colors to achieve the perfect hue!

BRAYER: A brayer is a handheld roller used to roll ink onto a block. For the projects in this book, I've used a small, soft-rubber brayer, which is ideal for fabric stamping because it distributes an even coat of ink, resulting in a crisp finished print.

CARVING BLOCK: Block printing can be done using any carvable surface. Common materials include linoleum, wood, Styrofoam, and even erasers. But my preference is a rubber carving block. These blocks cut like butter and are incredibly satisfying to work with. I particularly like the Speedy-Carve Soft Block made by Speedball; it is what I used for most of the block-printing projects in this book.

CARVING TOOLS: Block-printing—also called linocut—carving tools such as gouges and knives come in a variety of sizes and shapes. These special tools allow for precise carving of unwanted areas of the block. For every block-printed project in this book, I alternated between using a small V-tool, large V-tool, and large U-gouge. In my case, all the blades conveniently fit into the handle of the same tool, but you can also purchase these as individual tools.

BAREN: A baren (a pink one is shown in the center of the photo on the facing page) is a tool used to help apply even pressure when transferring the ink from the block to the fabric. I find it comfortable to use and feel that it helps deliver a consistent print. However, for all the projects in this book, because we are using small, soft-rubber blocks, it is completely optional. You can use your hands to apply pressure while printing and stamping instead.

FABRICS: While most of the projects in this book are stamped on premade fabric items, you will still want to consider fiber content and texture. Natural fabrics like cotton and linen absorb paint and ink nicely and work great for stamping. A smooth fabric with a tight weave will allow for a more precise and crisper look to your print. You'll also want to consider color. When working with acrylic craft paint, results will turn out best if the paint is darker than the fabric. So look for light, pale colors; white always works great! Fabric block-printing ink, on the other hand, is thicker than acrylic paint, so light ink colors still work well on darker fabrics. In general, keep in mind that you typically want to see contrast between the stamped image and the fabric.

PREPARING YOUR WORKSPACE

Before you dive into any project, you'll want to prepare your workspace. Make sure your space is large enough to accommodate your entire project. Typically, with fabric stamping, you want to have a firm but slightly padded surface. This helps to distribute even pressure when stamping. Layering sheets of fabric or laying fabric over quilt batting works well. I like to use a layer of parchment paper under my projects. But if you don't care about paint bleeding through to your layered fabrics, and the project can stay in place on your workspace until it fully dries, then skip the parchment paper. For most of the projects in this book, simply protecting your work surface with an old plastic tablecloth, plastic sheeting, or layered newsprint paper will suffice. Be sure to set up all the necessary tools and materials before you begin so they are all readily available.

Creative Color

As you can probably already tell from the look of this book, color is one of my favorite things! I absolutely love picking colors and putting together different color combinations. Whether you are drawn to bold, vibrant colors or prefer subtle, soft tones, selecting colors is an important step in your creations.

Let's take a moment to talk about the color wheel. It is a helpful tool that shows us basic colors, how they relate to one another, and how they can be mixed. The primary colors are red, blue, and yellow; these three colors are the foundation for creating all other colors. Mixing any two primary colors will produce the secondary colors, which are orange, green, and purple. If a primary color is mixed with the secondary color next to it, then a tertiary color is formed. Colors that are opposite each other on the wheel are known as complementary colors and always look great together.

Keep in mind that when using acrylic craft paints with textile medium, they will dry to a slightly different color than they look in the bottle. Always test your colors on scrap fabric first to make sure you will be happy with the result.

COLORS USED IN THE PROJECTS

Here is a list of all the paint colors I used throughout the book. If you are interested in re-creating something as closely as possible to how it appears in the photos, this is a good place to start—but by no means should you feel limited to these colors and brands!

ACRYLIC PAINT COLORS

- **Black**
  (Anita's All Purpose Acrylic Craft Paint)
- **White**
  (Anita's All Purpose Acrylic Craft Paint)
- **Christmas Red**
  (Anita's All Purpose Acrylic Craft Paint
- **Coral Cove**
  (Anita's All Purpose Acrylic Craft Paint)
- **Hunter Green**
  (Anita's All Purpose Acrylic Craft Paint)
- **Lavender**
  (Anita's All Purpose Acrylic Craft Paint)
- **Violet**
  (Deco Art Americana Acrylic Paint)
- **Sea Glass**
  (Deco Art Americana Acrylic Paint)
- **New Leaf Green**
  (Folk Art Matte Premium Acrylic Paint)
- **Raw Sienna**
  (Folk Art Matte Premium Acrylic Paint)
- **Teal**
  (Folk Art Matte Premium Acrylic Paint)
- **Terra Cotta**
  (Folk Art Matte Premium Acrylic Paint)
- **Warm Bisque**
  (Folk Art Matte Premium Acrylic Paint)
- **Windsor Blue**
  (Folk Art Matte Premium Acrylic Paint)
- **Yellow Ochre**
  (Folk Art Matte Premium Acrylic Paint)
- **Calypso Coral**
  (Delta Creative Ceramcoat Matte Acrylic Paint)

FABRIC INK COLORS (ALL SPEEDBALL)

- **Red**
- **White**
- **Black**
- **Green**
- **Blue**
- **Yellow**

THE COLOR WHEEL

Red

Red Violet

Red Orange

Violet

Orange

Blue Violet

Yellow Orange

Blue

Yellow

Blue Green

Yellow Green

Green

PRIMARY — SECONDARY — TERTIARY

Adapt & Play!

As you begin tackling the projects in this book, don't forget one very important fact: you can adapt different stamps to different fabric items. Don't feel limited to doing what I teach in a project. Choose stamps that you love and apply them to fabric items you'll use! As you can see on these pages, I tried the Folky Sunflower stamp on both a T-shirt and a tea towel, applied the Garter Snake stamp to a hardcover journal, and decorated another shirt with the Take Flight stamp that I originally designed for coasters. Use your imagination! Plus, these projects are great to do with kids—you can supervise and help to whatever level your little ones need, and they will be so proud of their result. I hope that this book will not only teach you solid techniques but also show you that you can apply them in many different ways. So don't forget to experiment and play!

CHAPTER 2:
The Basics of Fabric Stamping

This chapter includes detailed foundational tutorials for both foam stamping and block printing—two different stamp creation methods to choose from. Even if you prefer to use a different stamp pattern than the ones featured here, I highly recommend you practice each method by following these tutorials before tackling a full-blown project. Refer back to this detailed info as needed!

LABYRINTH

Foam stamping is a foolproof technique for stamping that delivers great results every time. The projects come out surprisingly clean and crisp. One of my favorite things about these craft foam stamps is that because they are mounted on acrylic glass, it's easy to see where you're stamping. You can easily restamp something if you didn't get it right the first time, which is nearly impossible with traditional stamps. I also love that you can make large-scale stamps. The cost is minimal and there are no special tools needed. Let's learn the basic technique for foam stamping!

TOOLS & MATERIALS

▶ Fabric; here, I've used a premade, prewashed 18" x 28" (45.7 x 71.1 cm) tea towel

▶ Labyrinth stamp pattern (page 157)

STAMPMAKING SUPPLIES

▶ Pencil

▶ Tracing paper

▶ Double-sided tape

▶ Craft foam with adhesive backing

▶ Bone folder paper creaser (optional)

▶ Scissors

▶ Craft knife

▶ Cutting mat

▶ 8½" x 11" (22 x 28 cm) sheet of acrylic glass

▶ Permanent marker

▶ Ruler/straightedge

▶ Safety glasses

PAINTING SUPPLIES

▶ Acrylic craft paint

▶ Textile medium

▶ Paint palette

▶ 1" (2.5 cm) craft foam brushes

▶ Craft paper/fabric/plastic

▶ Wet wipes or wet paper towels

▶ Baren (optional)

▶ Small paintbrush

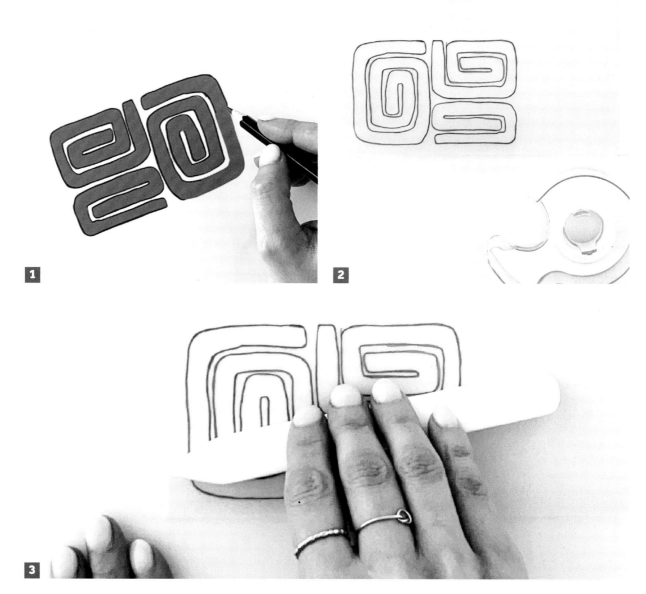

1. Trace the pattern. Secure a piece of tracing paper to the pattern using double-sided tape. Use a pencil to trace the pattern.

2. Tape down the tracing. Place the tracing face down (graphite side down) onto a piece of craft foam. Using double-sided tape, secure the tracing to the foam.

3. Transfer the tracing. Use a bone folder to transfer the pencil graphite to the foam. If you don't have a bone folder, try a wooden spoon or just use your fingers to rub the back of the tracing.

4. Check the transfer. Before fully removing the tracing paper, partially lift it up to make sure the graphite transferred well. If it didn't, lay the tracing paper back down and press down more firmly while rubbing the back of the tracing paper. If it still doesn't transfer, you might need to retrace the design, pressing down harder with your pencil.

5. Cut out the pattern. Cut out the pattern with scissors. Depending on the complexity of the design, you may need to switch to cutting out with a craft knife on top of a cutting mat. It's a good idea to have both on hand.

6. Draw the stamp base. Make a rectangle for your stamp to be mounted on. Use a ruler and permanent marker to draw lines indicating where to cut on a sheet of acrylic glass. Place the pattern underneath as a guide for sizing the stamp. For this project, I used a 4" x 5" (10 x 12.7 cm) rectangle. The key is simply to make the stamp a little larger than the design. Draw the longest cut line all the way across the entire sheet—this will be the line you cut first. (If you try to snap the glass only partly, the other side will crack.)

7. Score the cut lines. On the longest cut line, score the glass with a craft knife. Make three to five passes, gradually increasing the depth of the score with each pass. Just score the line—do not attempt to cut it all the way through.

8. Snap the first cut line. Wearing safety glasses, place both hands on either side of the scored line and snap the glass in half. If the glass does not

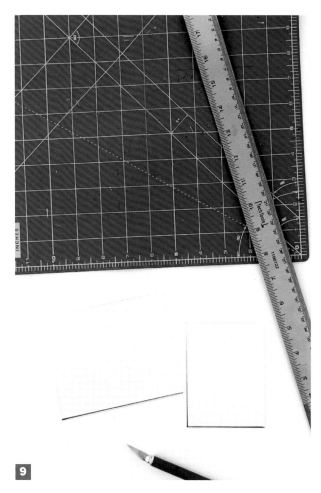

9

10

snap easily, make a few more passes with the craft knife.

9. Snap the second cut line. Repeat the process of scoring and snapping on the second cut line. Keep any excess rectangles of glass for later—during another project, you may find you can use these rectangles as stamp bases!

10. Adhere the pattern to the stamp base. Remove the paper backing from the adhesive side of the craft foam pattern pieces and press the pieces onto the glass stamp base. For some designs, you may want to place the tracing underneath the glass to help you align and position the foam pieces correctly.

SAFETY NOTE

Acrylic glass sheets purchased from the craft store are typically thin and very easy to work with. You will probably never "need" your safety glasses—I never saw a stray piece fly off when the glass was snapped—but you should always wear them anyway. If your glass is thicker, you may notice that the snapped edge is rough or even jagged. Sand this down with sandpaper if needed. Again, I never needed to do this when working with thin sheets from the craft store.

11

11. Mix paint with textile medium. With your chosen color, mix about 1 part acrylic craft paint to 2 parts textile medium. How much textile medium you add here can vary depending on the consistency of the paint and the look you're going for. Less textile medium will result in paint that looks thicker and more textured; it will also be closer in color to the raw paint. More textile medium will result in paint that looks more watery and is lighter in color. See the sidebar below.

COLOR AND TEXTILE MEDIUM

Here are three possible shades with differing ratios of paint to textile medium. The stamp on the far left is 1 part paint to 2 parts textile medium—which is the ratio I chose for the finished project. The stamp in the middle is closer to 1 part paint to 3 parts textile medium. And the stamp on the far right is 1 part paint to 4 parts textile medium.

12. Apply paint to the stamp. Prepare your workspace for stamping. Lay out craft paper, old fabric, or plastic to protect your work surface. Next, carefully dab your paint mixture onto your stamp using a foam brush. Make sure all the surfaces of your stamp are thoroughly and evenly coated. If you've chosen to use a ratio with less textile medium and more paint, how you load the paint can really affect the overall look. If you brush the paint onto the stamp instead of blotting it on, the result will look streakier. This is why it is important to do a test on scrap fabric before stamping on your actual project.

13. Prepare to stamp. Before you begin to stamp, clean up any drops of paint on the glass stamp base and any paint lingering on your hands. You don't want a smudge or a spot on your project! I like to keep wet wipes handy for this.

14

15

14. Test the stamp on a fabric scrap. If you haven't already, test out your stamp on a scrap of fabric. It is important to use the same fabric as your project, or at least something similar, because different fabrics absorb paint differently. When stamping, I like to use a block-printing baren to help apply even pressure. But you can use your hands if you don't have one. After stamping the test, make any adjustments you wish: adding more paint or textile medium to the paint, applying more even pressure when stamping, loading the paint onto the stamp differently, etc. You may find that your stamp needs a modification; if so, clean it off with soap and water and make the adjustment needed.

15. Apply the first stamp. Decide on the pattern layout for your project. Do you want a random pattern? A spaced-out grid? A staggered arrangement? Full coverage or partial coverage? The possibilities are endless. Depending on your desired look, the specific stamp, and the project, you might need to do some planning and measuring before you start stamping, especially if you're stamping on a premade project like a place mat or tea towel. For this particular project and pattern, just jump right in and begin stamping in the bottom right-hand corner.

16. Continue stamping. You will need to reload with paint after every stamp. I like to work from right to left and from bottom to top. For the most part, I prefer to eyeball the placement. This is why I love having a clear stamp base—it makes placing the stamp much easier. For this project, if you want to follow along with my arrangement, offset the stamp by half of the stamp's width when stamping the next row above the previous row, as opposed to placing the stamp exactly aligned with the previous row. As you can see, the two small swirls are over the one bigger swirl in the second row.

17. Clean up the stamping. This last step is totally optional. Using a small paintbrush and a dabbing motion, lightly fill in some of the spots that didn't get enough paint. On one hand, I do love the hand-stamped look; all the imperfections add character and charm. On the other hand, for this project, I'm stamping on premade tea towels, and the seams of the hem stand out. While I don't mind the look of that too much, I thought filling it in a bit would look a little more polished. Plus, I find the process to be very relaxing, like coloring in a coloring book. When you're completely done, wash the stamp, paintbrush, and other supplies with liquid dish soap and water.

WOODLAND MUSHROOM

Block printing is the process of carving a relief into a block, applying ink to the raised areas of the block, and then pressing the block onto fabric to transfer the design. The lovely imperfections unique to block printing add character and handmade charm to fabric. The process of carving a block can be time consuming, but it tends to be relaxing and calming. And, once the block is carved, it's incredibly satisfying to see the finished design printed on fabric. Let's learn the basic technique for block printing!

TOOLS & MATERIALS

- Fabric; here, I've used a premade, prewashed 18" x 28" (45.7 x 71.1 cm) tea towel
- Woodland Mushroom stamp pattern (page 162)

STAMPMAKING SUPPLIES

- Tracing paper
- Pencil
- Double-sided tape
- Rubber carving block
- Bone folder paper creaser (optional)
- Permanent marker
- Carving tools
- Scissors
- Craft knife (optional)
- Cutting mat (optional)
- Rubbing alcohol
- Paper towel
- Craft paper/fabric/plastic
- Paper plate or paint palette

PAINTING SUPPLIES

- Fabric ink; here, I've used Speedball green, black, and blue
- Palette knife
- 8" x 10" (20.3 x 25.4 cm) sheet of acrylic glass, baking sheet, or other flat surface
- Soft-rubber brayer
- Wet wipes or wet paper towels
- Baren (optional)
- Small paintbrush
- Cardstock (optional)

TRANSFERRING THE PATTERN

1. Trace the pattern. Secure a piece of tracing paper to the pattern using double-sided tape. Use a pencil to trace the pattern.

2. Transfer the tracing. Remove the tracing from the pattern. Then place the tracing face down (graphite side down) onto a 4" x 6" (10 x 15.2 cm) carving block. Using double-sided tape, secure the tracing to the block. Use a bone folder to transfer the pencil graphite to the block. If you don't have a bone folder, try a wooden spoon or just use your fingers to rub the back of the tracing.

3. Check the transfer. Before fully removing the tracing paper, partially lift it up to make sure the graphite transferred well. If it didn't, lay the tracing paper back down and press down more firmly while rubbing the back of the tracing paper. If it still doesn't transfer, you might need to retrace the design, pressing down harder with your pencil.

COLORING AND CARVING THE PATTERN

4. Color in the negative space. Use a black permanent marker to start filling in all the areas that will be cut. Remember: the cut-away parts will be the negative space in the design, and the untouched/raised parts will be the stamped design. So think in reverse: you're coloring in the opposite areas, or the places that will remain white.

5. Finishing coloring in. Color about ¼" to ½" (0.6 to 1.3 cm) around the outside of the entire pattern. I like this step because it helps prevent you from making any mistakes when carving. If you carve away the wrong thing, it can't be fixed, but if you mess up with the marker, it can still be fixed! You don't need to fill in the entire area around the design that you plan to cut away—but at least make this clear, bold outline around the entire shape.

6. Begin carving. Smaller blades make more-precise cuts and remove less of the block; larger blades are less exact but remove more of the block more quickly. The blades are sharp, so, when carving, always keep the blade facing away from your body. Start with the smallest blade on the outline of the design. Try to keep the handle at about a 45-degree angle and the blade parallel to the block. The blade should smoothly cut the rubber block.

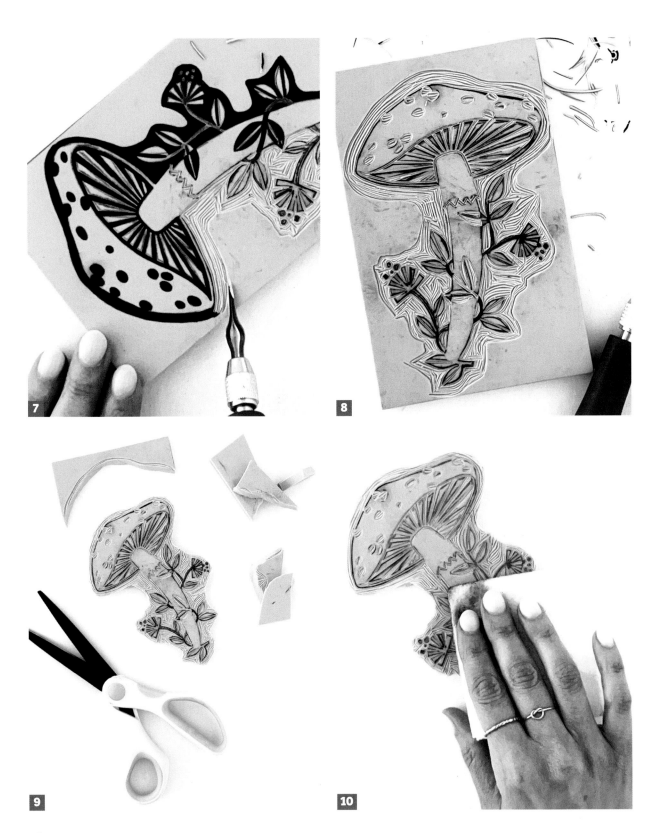

7. Continue carving. Go slow and take your time; you don't want to make a mistake here, because it can't be fixed. Once you get a feel for the tools and the design, play around with the different blades to see what works for you. I usually end up rotating between three blades.

8. Finish carving. Keep going until you've cut all or most of the black from the marker away. As you can see here, you may not need to cut off every single speck if your marker overcolored certain areas. Use your fingers and eyes to check the final effect.

9. Cut away the excess. Cut away all areas of the block that are outside the final shape using either scissors or a craft knife and cutting mat.

10. Clean up the marker. Use rubbing alcohol on a paper towel to remove any excess marker ink from the stamp.

PREPARING THE INK

11

12

11. Prepare your workspace and ink. Lay out craft paper, old fabric, or plastic to protect your work surface. Then mix your ink colors on a paper plate or paint palette. For this project, I knew I wanted the green to be a little cooler and a little darker, so I added a bit of blue and black to it. I started with about a tablespoon of green, a teaspoon of blue, and a half-teaspoon of black.

12. Finalize your ink color. Mix the inks with a palette knife. Here I added a bit more blue and black ink to the mixture. The color-mixing process can include some trial and error; continue adding small amounts of different inks until you are satisfied with the color.

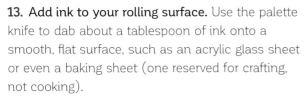

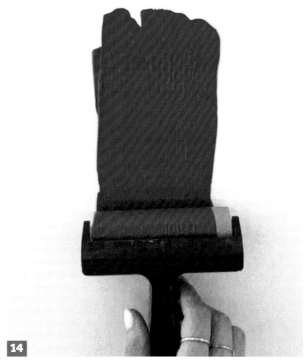

13. Add ink to your rolling surface. Use the palette knife to dab about a tablespoon of ink onto a smooth, flat surface, such as an acrylic glass sheet or even a baking sheet (one reserved for crafting, not cooking).

14. First, roll the ink vertically. Use a brayer to pull the ink down in a vertical motion. Roll from top to bottom, spreading the ink.

15. Next, roll the ink horizontally. Continue rolling up and down and side to side. This ink on the sheet is called an ink well. The goal is to create a nice, even coat of ink on the brayer.

16

17

18

16. Check your brayer. To know when you are ready to stamp, you need to check your brayer. Shown here is how you do NOT want your brayer to look—it's not ready yet. This is not an even coat of ink. Note how the ink in the middle of the roller has a long, globby texture; this is too much ink, and there is not enough ink on the near side (closest to the camera).

17. Keep rolling until the brayer is ready. Continue rolling up and down and side to side. In this picture, you can see that there is a thin, even coat of ink with very little texture. It reminds me of what a wall looks like when you first roll wet paint onto it. You'll know your ink is ready when you start to hear a tacky sound while rolling.

18. Clean your hands. Use wet wipes or wet paper towels to make sure your hands are clean before you start handling your fabric item.

TESTING THE STAMP

19. Ink the stamp. Using your well-prepared brayer, fill your stamp block with ink. Roll the ink up and down and side to side on the block. You're aiming for a thin, even coat of ink on the block.

20. Test the stamp. On a scrap of fabric (preferably the same fabric as your project), test out your stamp. Testing the block helps prime the block, making for a much-better finished product. I like to use a baren to help apply even pressure, but you can just use your hands if you don't have one. In this photo, you can see all the little lines around the mushroom that were left when carving. I love having a little bit of this because it adds to the charming, handmade look of the stamp. But, in this case, it's a little more than I want, so I'd like to remove some of them.

21. Adjust the stamp. Wash your block with liquid dish soap and water and carve away anything else you don't want. With a little bit of ink residue left on the stamp, it's easier to see what to remove!

22. Test the adjusted stamp. Load your stamp with ink. On scrap fabric, test your stamp again. In this picture you can see the difference between the first test (left) and the second text (right). There are still some little extra lines for charm, but the effect is somewhat tidier.

23. Stamp your project. You're finally ready to print! If you are printing on a tea towel like the one here, find the center by folding it in half lengthwise and then creasing the fabric with your hand. Load the stamp with ink and place it in the center of the crease line about 2½" (6.4 cm) from the bottom. Apply even pressure with your hand or a baren, then carefully remove the block. If you want to do any touch-ups to the print, use a small paintbrush and a dabbing motion to lightly fill in any spots that didn't get enough ink.

24. Use up the rest of the ink. If you have enough ink left over on your rolling sheet, try making a quick print on cardstock! When you're completely done, wash the stamp, paintbrush, and other supplies with liquid dish soap and water.

22

STAMPING THE PROJECT

23

24

CHAPTER 3:
Foam-Stamping Projects

Here are 9 foam-stamping projects to build your skills as well as your stamp stash! You'll learn to create complex patterns, layers of color, multi-stamp arrangements, and more in this chapter. If your home isn't full of stamped tea towels, napkins, place mats, and pillowcases by the time you're through this book, I'll be surprised!

If needed, refer to the foundational foam-stamping tutorial on pages 28–37 for more technical guidance on executing the project steps.

COLORFUL COSMO TEA TOWEL

This is a perfect starter project! It is simple but colorful and teaches precision in the cutting, assembling, and applying of the stamp. The stamp pattern, with its seven separate petals, offers tons of latitude for color customization, and the overall round shape means you can create many different arrangements across large surfaces like a tea towel or table runner.

TOOLS & MATERIALS

- 18" x 28" (45.7 x 71.1 cm) premade, prewashed white cotton tea towel
- Colorful Cosmo stamp pattern (page 155)

STAMPMAKING SUPPLIES

- Pencil
- Tracing paper
- Double-sided tape
- Craft foam with adhesive backing
- Bone folder paper creaser (optional)
- Scissors
- Craft knife
- Cutting mat
- 8½" x 11" (22 x 28 cm) sheet of acrylic glass, or scraps of sufficient size (refer to pattern)
- Permanent marker
- Ruler/straightedge
- Safety glasses

PAINTING SUPPLIES

- Acrylic craft paint in 8 colors: Black, Christmas Red, Violet, Lavender, Sea Glass, Calypso Coral, Raw Sienna, Hunter Green
- Textile medium
- Paint palette
- Craft foam brushes
- Craft paper/fabric/plastic
- Wet wipes or wet paper towels
- Baren (optional)
- Small paintbrush (optional)

There are tons of color customization possibilities with this stamp design!

1. **Trace.** Tape a piece of tracing paper to the pattern provided. Use a pencil to trace the pattern.

2. **Transfer.** Tape the tracing, face down, to a piece of foam. Then transfer the pencil graphite to the foam using a bone folder or other tool.

3. **Check.** Remove the tracing, making sure the graphite transferred.

4. **Start cutting out.** Cut out around the outside of the flower pattern using scissors.

5. **Cut out the details.** Cut out the details using a craft knife: the individual petals, the lines inside the petals, and the blobs in the flower center.

6. **Mount the main design.** Make an acrylic glass stamp base to fit the flower. Peel off the paper backing from the foam and stick the petals only onto the glass. Use the pattern under the glass as a guide if needed.

5

7. **Mount the details.** Use the edge of a craft knife or a pair of tweezers to place the tiny pieces in the center of the flower.

8. **Mix paint.** Mix each of the paint colors with textile medium. I used a different color for each petal and mixed them in order in my palette. I used black for the flower center blobs, which I had to mix in a separate palette because I ran out of palette spots!

9. **Prep the stamp.** Once you have mixed each color, load your stamp with paint. Switch to a small paintbrush if you are worried about accidentally getting the wrong color in an area.

10. **Test the stamp.** Prepare your workspace for stamping. On a scrap of fabric, test the stamp. Make any adjustments to the stamp that you see are needed.

6

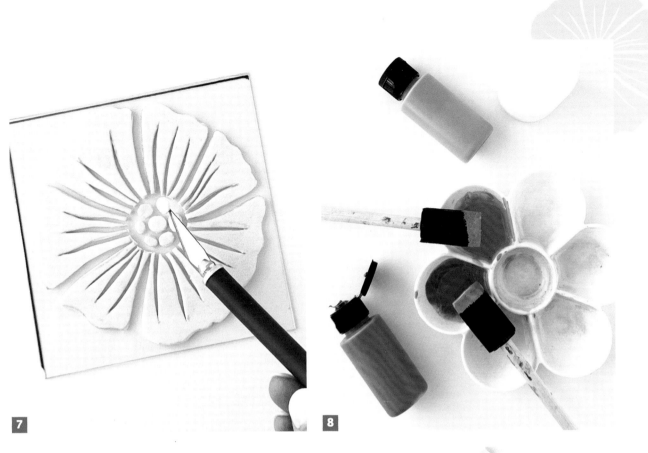

11. Begin stamping. When the stamp is ready, load it with paint again and stamp the tea towel in the bottom right corner. Continue stamping by placing the next stamp about three fingers-width apart from the previously placed stamp. When you begin the next row above the first, align the stamp between the two flowers below, creating a checkerboard-like pattern.

12. Touch up. Finish by using a small paintbrush to touch up any areas that need a bit more paint.

Try simplifying your color scheme to just two solid-color cosmos that alternate in a checkerboard pattern. The design will come together really quickly!

PATTERN VARIATION IDEAS

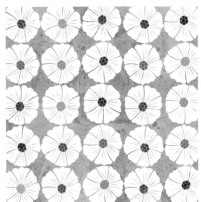

ARC TEA TOWEL

In this project, you'll branch out to using two separate stamps to create your design. This not only makes repeat stamping faster and easier but also allows for more variation and creativity. And, because you're creating two separate stamps, this also means you can use just the arc stamp to create cool abstract or rainbow designs for a different project.

TOOLS & MATERIALS

▶ 18" x 28" (45.7 x 71.1 cm) premade, prewashed white cotton tea towel
▶ Arc stamp pattern (page 158)

STAMPMAKING SUPPLIES

▶ Pencil
▶ Tracing paper
▶ Double-sided tape
▶ Craft foam with adhesive backing
▶ Bone folder paper creaser (optional)
▶ Scissors
▶ Craft knife
▶ Cutting mat
▶ 8½" x 11" (22 x 28 cm) sheet of acrylic glass, or scraps of sufficient size (refer to pattern)
▶ Permanent marker
▶ Ruler/straightedge
▶ Safety glasses

PAINTING SUPPLIES

▶ Acrylic craft paint in 3 colors: Black, Sea Glass, Violet
▶ Textile medium
▶ Paint palette
▶ Craft foam brushes
▶ Craft paper/fabric/plastic
▶ Wet wipes or wet paper towels
▶ Baren (optional)
▶ Small paintbrush (optional)

This project uses two separate stamps, which means the stamps can be adapted in creative ways.

1. **Trace.** Tape a piece of tracing paper to the pattern provided. Use a pencil to trace the pattern.

2. **Transfer.** Tape the tracing, face down, to a piece of foam. Then transfer the pencil graphite to the foam using a bone folder or other tool.

3. **Check.** Remove the tracing, making sure the graphite transferred.

4. **Cut out the main shape.** Cut the three main sections of the design out using scissors—the dots, the petals, and the stem.

5. **Cut out the details.** Finishing cutting out the individual pieces and details using a craft knife.

6. **Mount the petals.** Make two acrylic glass stamp bases to fit the design—one will be for the petals, and one will be for the dots and stem. Peel off the paper backing from the foam and stick the flower petal pieces onto one stamp base. Use the pattern under the glass as a guide if needed.

7. **Mount the dots and stem.** Mount the dots and stem on the second stamp base, using the pattern under the glass as a guide to ensure that your two separate stamps will work together correctly. Use the edge of a craft knife or a pair or tweezers to help place the small dots.

8. **Mix paint.** Mix each of the paint colors with textile medium.

9. **Prep the stamps.** Once you have mixed each color, load your stamps with paint, using a different brush for each color.

10. **Test the stamps.** Prepare your workspace for stamping. On a scrap of fabric, test the stamps, first stamping the petals and then stamping the stem and dots. Make any adjustments to the stamps that you see are needed. Practice aligning the two stamps correctly if you are having trouble.

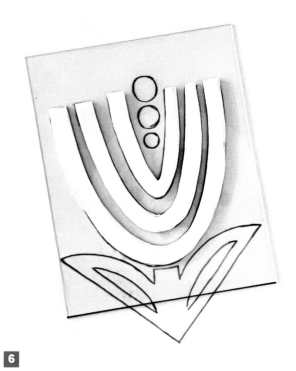

6

7

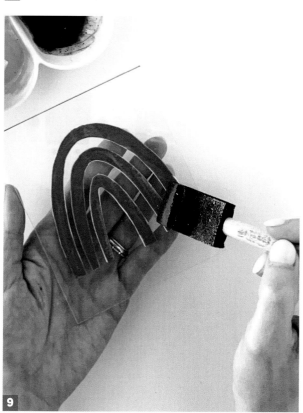

9

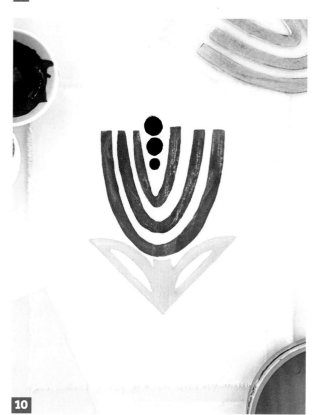

10

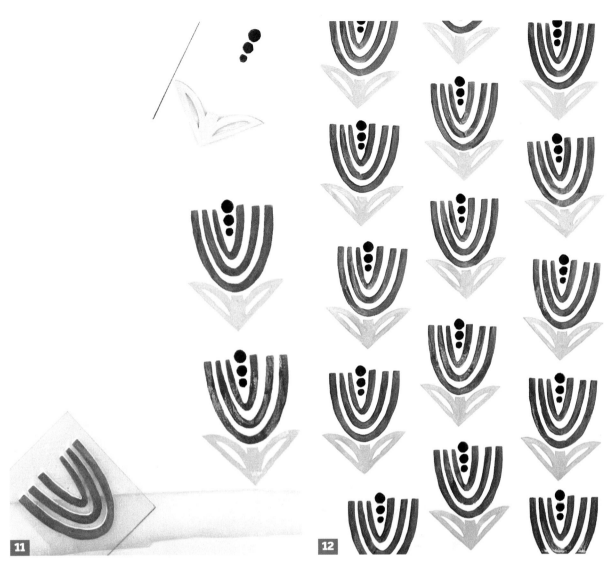

11. Start stamping. When the stamps are ready, load them with paint again and begin stamping your tea towel in the bottom right corner. Continue stamping vertically along the edge of the towel, placing the next stamp directly above the previous stamp with just a bit of space between them. When you begin the next row to the left, align the first stamp between the two flowers to the right in order to create a staggered effect.

12. Touch up. Finish by using a small paintbrush to touch up any areas that need a bit more paint.

Try using just the arc stamp to make a series of black (or multicolored) rainbows! Layering stamps are so much fun to find new applications for.

PATTERN VARIATION IDEAS

SUNBURST TEA TOWEL

Another two-stamp design, this project teaches how to carefully align your stamps into a more complex pattern. The circle stamp can be used in so many other projects too—you'll definitely find yourself reaching for it again!

TOOLS & MATERIALS

- 18" x 28" (45.7 x 71.1 cm) premade, prewashed white cotton tea towel
- Sunburst stamp pattern (page 156)

STAMPMAKING SUPPLIES

- Pencil
- Tracing paper
- Double-sided tape
- Craft foam with adhesive backing
- Bone folder paper creaser (optional)
- Scissors
- Craft knife
- Cutting mat
- 8½" x 11" (22 x 28 cm) sheet of acrylic glass, or scraps of sufficient size (refer to pattern)
- Permanent marker
- Ruler/straightedge
- Safety glasses

PAINTING SUPPLIES

- Acrylic craft paint in 2 colors: Black, Raw Sienna
- Textile medium
- Paint palette
- Craft foam brushes
- Craft paper/fabric/plastic
- Wet wipes or wet paper towels
- Baren (optional)
- Small paintbrush (optional)

Like the Arc Tea Towel project, this project uses two separate stamps for maximum design flexibility.

1. **Trace.** Tape a piece of tracing paper to the pattern provided. Use a pencil to trace the pattern.

2. **Transfer.** Tape the tracing, face down, to a piece of foam. Then transfer the pencil graphite to the foam using a bone folder or other tool.

3. **Check.** Remove the tracing, making sure the graphite transferred.

4. **Cut out.** Cut out the sunburst and circle using a craft knife and/or scissors.

5. **Mount.** Make two stamp bases out of acrylic glass to fit both the sunburst and the circle. Peel off the paper backing from the foam and stick the shapes onto the glass. Use the pattern under the glass as a guide if needed.

6. **Mix paint.** Mix the black paint with textile medium.

1

7. **Prep and test the stamp.** Prepare your workspace for stamping. Load your sunburst stamp with paint. On a scrap of fabric, test the stamp. Make any adjustments to the stamp that you see are needed.

8. **Start stamping.** When the stamp is ready, begin stamping the tea towel. Start by placing the stamp in the bottom right-hand corner, allowing about half of the stamp to be cropped off. Add more paint to the bottom of the stamp, rotate the stamp 180 degrees so the sunburst is facing down instead of up, then place the stamp just to the left of the first sunburst so the ends meet, allowing the sunburst to be cropped off. Continue stamping in this pattern across an entire row, then continue to create more rows, filling the tea towel.

4

9. Prep the second stamp. Once you've stamped the whole tea towel with the sunburst design, mix the Raw Sienna paint with textile medium. Prep and test the circle stamp.

10. Continue stamping. Add circles in between the sunbursts. If needed, finish the design by using a small paintbrush to touch up any areas that need a bit more paint.

VARIATION: BICOLOR SUNBURSTS

You can create a totally different look by omitting the circle stamp and just creating mirrored rows in two colors with the sunburst stamp. If you plan to apply all rows of one color first, make sure you measure the space and stagger the rows so that the design turns out neat.

Here's one more tea towel for the road! These tea towels feature just one stamp that can be staggered in rows (like the red towel) or mirrored in columns (like the brown and pink towel). Find this bonus foam stamp pattern on page 157.

BOLD BLOSSOM NAPKINS

This project is a favorite among the friends and family who have come into my studio. It's a multi-stamp, multi-layer, colorful design that, despite its complexity, is actually pretty easy to nail. Just take your time cutting and assembling the different stamps, stay organized, and you'll have amazing results in no time.

TOOLS & MATERIALS

- 20" x 20" (50.8 x 50.8 cm) premade, prewashed white cotton napkins
- Bold Blossom stamp pattern (page 164)

STAMPMAKING SUPPLIES

- Pencil
- Tracing paper
- Double-sided tape
- Craft foam with adhesive backing
- Bone folder paper creaser (optional)
- Scissors
- Craft knife
- Cutting mat
- 8½" x 11" (22 x 28 cm) sheet of acrylic glass
- Permanent marker
- Ruler/straightedge
- Safety glasses

PAINTING SUPPLIES

- Acrylic craft paint in 6 colors: Black, Christmas Red, Violet, New Leaf Green, Warm Bisque, Sea Glass
- Textile medium
- Paint palette
- Craft foam brushes
- Craft paper/fabric/plastic
- Wet wipes or wet paper towels
- Baren (optional)
- Small paintbrush (optional)

This showstopping design is built using six layered stamps.

1. **Trace.** Tape a piece of tracing paper to the pattern provided. Use a pencil to trace the pattern.

2. **Transfer.** Tape the tracing, face down, to a piece of foam. Then transfer the pencil graphite to the foam using a bone folder or other tool.

3. **Check and start cutting out.** Remove the tracing, making sure the graphite transferred. Then cut out the large pieces of the pattern using scissors.

4. **Cut the details.** Cut out the small details, like the leaf vein and the stamens, using a craft knife.

5. **Start mounting.** Make acrylic glass stamp bases to fit each element. The two leaves should be a single stamp, as should the stamens and stem. Peel off the paper backing from the foam and stick the pieces onto the glass. Use the pattern under the glass as a guide if needed.

6. **Finish mounting.** In the end, you should have four petal stamps, one leaves stamp, and one stamens and stem stamp.

7. **Mix paint.** Mix the red paint with textile medium.

8. **Prep the first stamp.** Load the widest petal stamp (the bottom one, #1) with paint.

9. **Test the first stamp.** Prepare your workspace for stamping. On a scrap of fabric, test the stamp.

10. **Prep and test the remaining petals.** Repeat the process to mix paint, prep, and test the other three petal stamps, doing #2, then #3, and finally #4. Allow the paint to dry to the touch in between each layer.

3

4

12

11. Prep and test the stem. Next, stamp the stamens and stem. Line up the top of the stem half with the bottom of the flower.

12. Prep and test the leaves. Finally, stamp the leaves. Make any adjustments to any of the stamps that you see are needed.

13

13. Prepare the fabric. When the stamps are ready, find the center of the napkin by folding it in half lengthwise, then creasing the fabric with your hand.

14. Start stamping. Start stamping in the center of the napkin, with the middle of the flower and the stem aligned nearly on the crease. Petal #1 should start about 4" (10 cm) from the bottom of the napkin. If you are stamping more than one napkin, lay them all out, then stamp petal #1 on all the napkins, then petal #2, etc. This will cut down on drying time.

15. Touch up. After you've stamped all the layers, use a small paintbrush to touch up any areas that need a bit more paint. This step is important for this project because of the layered stamping. Paint absorbs into fabric but sits on top of already-painted fabric. Dabbing a little more paint onto the layered areas adds a nice, smooth finish.

15

You can also make napkins using the block-printing technique! To make these napkins, simply follow the foundational block-printing tutorial on page 38 and apply the stamp in a repeating, aligned pattern. Find this bonus block-printing stamp pattern on page 162.

PATTERN VARIATION IDEAS

MOD FLOWER PLACE MATS

It's time to break away from the tea towels! In truth, most projects in this book can be adapted to different fabric bases; here's one on a place mat! In this project, we'll incorporate a new tool to add detail: a sponge dauber.

TOOLS & MATERIALS

- 14" x 19" (35.6 x 48.3 cm) premade, prewashed white cotton place mats
- Mod Flower stamp pattern (page 167)

STAMPMAKING SUPPLIES

- Pencil
- Tracing paper
- Double-sided tape
- Craft foam with adhesive backing
- Bone folder paper creaser (optional)
- Scissors
- Craft knife
- Cutting mat
- 8½" x 11" (22 x 28 cm) sheet of acrylic glass, or scraps of sufficient size (refer to pattern)
- Permanent marker
- Ruler/straightedge
- Safety glasses

PAINTING SUPPLIES

- Acrylic craft paint in 2 colors: Black, New Leaf Green
- Textile medium
- Paint palette
- Craft foam brushes
- Craft paper/fabric/plastic
- Wet wipes or wet paper towels
- Baren (optional)
- ¼" (0.6 cm) sponge dauber
- Small paintbrush (optional)

Use a paint dauber to quickly and easily add the yellow dots to this design!

1. **Trace.** Tape a piece of tracing paper to the pattern provided. Use a pencil to trace the pattern.

2. **Transfer.** Tape the tracing, face down, to a piece of foam. Then transfer the pencil graphite to the foam using a bone folder or other tool.

3. **Check.** Remove the tracing, making sure the graphite transferred.

4. **Cut out.** Cut out the flower using scissors and a craft knife. Pay close attention to how the center should be cut out by referring to this photo.

5. **Mount.** Make an acrylic glass stamp base to fit the flower. Peel off the paper backing from the foam and stick it onto the glass. Use the pattern under the glass as a guide if needed.

6. **Mix paint.** Mix the black paint with textile medium.

4

7. **Prep and test the stamp.** Prepare your workspace for stamping. Load your stamp with paint. On a scrap of fabric, test the stamp. Make any adjustments to the stamp that you see are needed.

8. **Start stamping.** Because this stamp is so large and the place mat is rather small, you'll want the stamp placement to be quite even. Find the center of the place mat by folding it in half, meeting corners to corners, and then crease it with your hand. Place the first stamp in the center of that crease line, cropping about ½" (1.3 cm) of it off the bottom of the place mat. Reload the stamp with paint and place it, partially rotated, just to the right of the first stamp, aligning the tops of the flowers and leaving about a ¼" (0.6 cm) or one finger-width between the two stamps. Repeat on the left side.

5

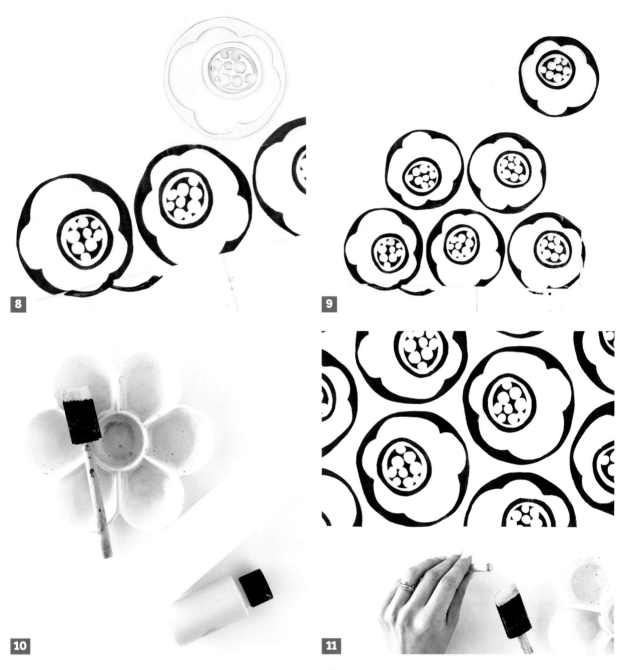

9. Continue stamping. When you begin the next row above, stagger each flower between the two flowers on the row below. Make sure you continue to rotate the flower each time so the pattern looks more organic. Crop the stamp off the edge of the place mat as needed along the sides. Fill the entire place mat.

10. Mix paint. It's time for the flower centers! Mix the New Leaf Green paint with textile medium.

11. Prep the dauber. Add this yellow-green paint to the sponge dauber using a foam brush.

12. Stamp dots. Stamp dots inside each of the open circles in the center of each flower.

13. Repeat. Repeat this for all the flowers. Finish by using a small paintbrush to touch up any areas that need a bit more paint. I didn't need to do any cleanup for this project—my flowers came out very crisp!

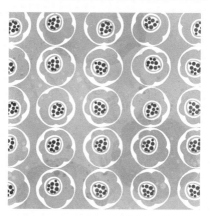

CHEERFUL BLOOMS PILLOWCASE

This project will challenge you with its complex, multi-layered, multi-stamp elements and some freehand fabric painting. But it's completely achievable because it simply builds up in stages and layers. You'll learn to use painter's tape to create easy guidelines and how to use unexpected tools—like the tip of a paintbrush—as stamps too!

TOOLS & MATERIALS

- 16" x 16" (40.6 x 40.6 cm) premade, prewashed white cotton canvas pillowcase
- Cheerful Blooms stamp pattern (page 163)

STAMPMAKING SUPPLIES

- Pencil
- Tracing paper
- Double-sided tape
- Craft foam with adhesive backing
- Bone folder paper creaser (optional)
- Scissors
- Craft knife
- Cutting mat
- ¼" (0.6 cm) (standard-sized) hole punch
- 8½" x 11" (22 x 28 cm) sheet of acrylic glass, or scraps of sufficient size (refer to pattern)
- Permanent marker
- Ruler/straightedge
- Safety glasses

PAINTING SUPPLIES

- Parchment paper or cardboard
- Acrylic craft paint in 10 colors: Black, Christmas Red, Hunter Green, New Leaf Green, Sea Glass, Raw Sienna, Calypso Coral, Coral Cove, Violet, Lavender
- Textile medium
- Paint palette
- Craft foam brushes
- Craft paper/fabric/plastic
- Wet wipes or wet paper towels
- Baren (optional)
- ½" (1.3 cm) sponge dauber
- ¼" (0.6 cm) sponge dauber
- Painter's tape
- Small paintbrush

1. **Trace.** Tape a piece of tracing paper to the pattern provided. Use a pencil to trace the pattern. I used ½" (1.3 cm) sponge daubers for the center of the flowers. If you don't have these, you can make a little circle stamp using the pattern.

2. **Transfer.** Tape the tracing, face down, to a piece of foam. Then transfer the pencil graphite to the foam using a bone folder or other tool.

3. **Check and cut out.** Remove the tracing, making sure the graphite transferred. Then cut out the flowers and larger pieces using scissors.

4. **Finish cutting out.** Cut out the holes and flower details using a craft knife.

5. **Punch dots.** Use a standard-sized hole punch to punch a bunch of little dots—eight of them.

6. **Mount.** Make seven acrylic glass stamp bases to fit the design as shown. The four small leaves should be a single stamp and the eight dots should be a single stamp. Peel off the paper backing from the foam and stick the pieces onto the glass. Use the pattern under the glass as a guide if needed. Use the edge of a craft knife or a pair of tweezers to help place tiny pieces.

7. **Mix paint.** Mix the Calypso Coral paint with textile medium.

8. **Prep and test the first stamp.** Prepare your workspace for stamping. Load the first stamp—the largest flower—with paint. On a scrap of fabric, test the stamp. Make any adjustments to the stamp that you see are needed.

9. **Stamp the first flower.** Find the center of your pillowcase by folding it in half lengthwise, meeting corners to corners, then creasing the fabric with your hand. Place parchment paper or cardboard inside to protect the backside of the pillowcase.

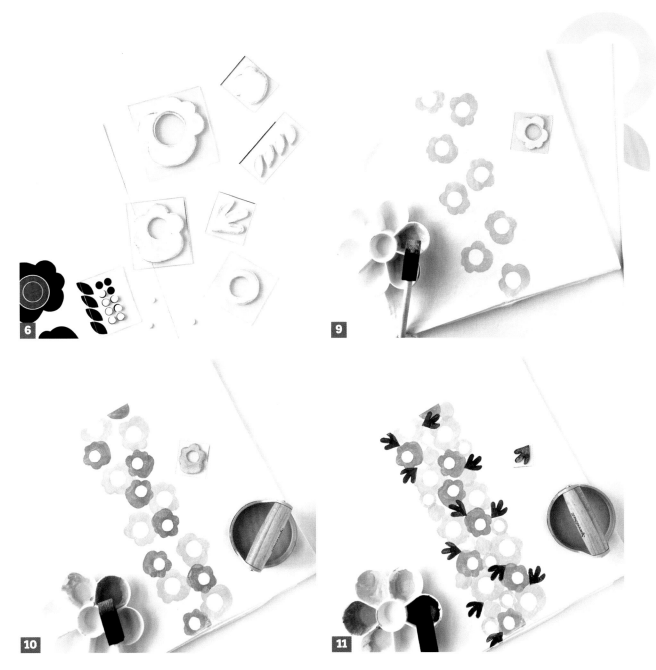

Begin stamping with the largest flower stamp, staggering it all along the creased line.

10. Stamp the second flower. Mix textile medium with Lavender paint. Test the smaller flower stamp on scrap fabric. Make any adjustments you see are needed. Then begin stamping on the pillowcase, placing this flower in between the larger flowers. The placement doesn't need to be perfect. Consider the overall balance rather than precision.

11. Stamp the leaves, small flowers, and rings. Repeat this process with three more stamps. Start with the larger stamp and work your way to the smallest—so, do the solid flower, then the ring, then the leaves. Stamp along the center of the pillowcase, placing the stamps within 2" (5 cm) of either side of the crease line and overlapping them slightly.

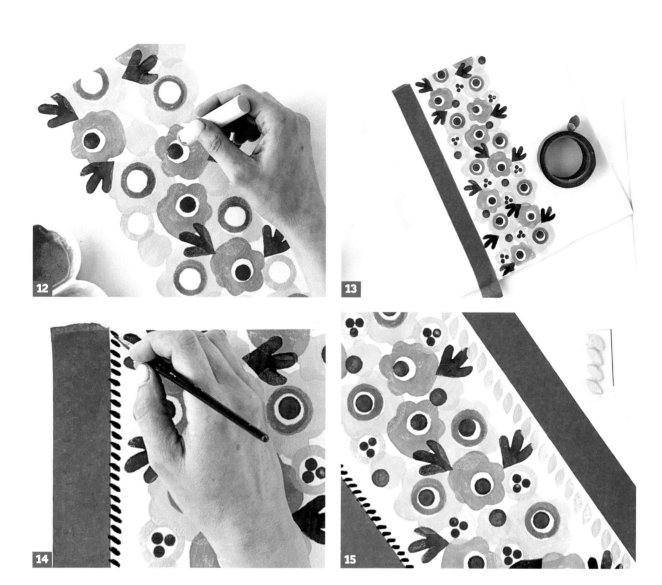

12. Add more rings and dots. Go back in with the ring stamp to add coral rings to the centers of the largest flowers. Then use a ½" (1.3 cm) sponge dauber to stamp the middle of the smaller flowers. Apply paint to the sponge dauber with a sponge brush, then stamp. Reapply the paint to the sponge dauber every third stamp or so. Repeat this to also add dots to the middle of the largest flowers (shown in the step 13 photo). Finally, use a ¼" (0.6 cm) sponge dauber to add three dots to the centers of the floating rings (shown in the step 13 photo).

13. Create a guideline. Place painter's tape along the left side of the flower column. Leave about ½" or ¾" (1.3 or 2 cm) between the edge of most of the flowers and the tape. It is okay if some of the flowers slightly overlap the tape.

14. Add freehand marks. Mix the black paint with textile medium. With a small, flat paintbrush, make little slanted dash marks along the right (inner) side of the tape.

15. Stamp mini leaves. Place painter's tape along the right side of the flower column, leaving a slightly larger gap on this side than you did on the

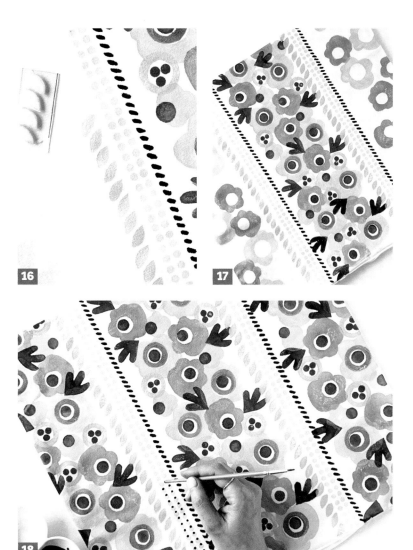

left side. Use the mini leaves stamp to stamp a column of leaves along the left (inner) side of the tape.

16. Stamp dots and more leaves and dashes. Remove the painter's tape. Then stamp the sets of little dots along the outside of the columns of dashes and leaves. Next, add a column of mini leaves along the left side and a column of freehand dashes along the right side (shown in the step 17 photo).

17. Add more flowers. Repeat the main flower column pattern on both outside edges of the pillowcase. Follow the same sequence: start with the main flowers (shown), then build up the additional layers (shown in the step 18 photo).

18. Add final details. Add tiny black dots on top of the yellow dots using the end of a small paintbrush. Finish by using a small paintbrush to touch up any areas that need a bit more paint.

PATTERN VARIATION IDEAS

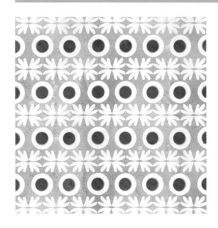

SCALLOP SHELL PILLOWCASE

There's something simple but elegant about this design. As you execute it, you'll hone your alignment skills, learn to embrace imperfection and stamp overlap, and do some more dramatic freehand fabric painting. (Or you can give yourself a break with a painter's tape guideline while freehand painting—it's up to you!)

TOOLS & MATERIALS

▸ 12" x 20" (30.5 x 50.8 cm) premade, prewashed white cotton canvas pillowcase

▸ Scallop Shell stamp pattern (page 167)

STAMPMAKING SUPPLIES

▸ Pencil

▸ Tracing paper

▸ Double-sided tape

▸ Craft foam with adhesive backing

▸ Bone folder paper creaser (optional)

▸ Scissors

▸ Craft knife

▸ Cutting mat

▸ 8½" x 11" (22 x 28 cm) sheet of acrylic glass

▸ Permanent marker

▸ Ruler/straightedge

▸ Safety glasses

PAINTING SUPPLIES

▸ Parchment paper or cardboard

▸ Acrylic craft paint in 2 colors: Black, Teal

▸ Textile medium

▸ Paint palette

▸ Craft foam brushes

▸ Craft paper/fabric/plastic

▸ Wet wipes or wet paper towels

▸ Baren (optional)

▸ Small paintbrush (optional)

Enjoy the challenge of a bit of freehand drawing in this project.

1. **Trace.** Tape a piece of tracing paper to the pattern provided. Use a pencil to trace the pattern.

2. **Transfer.** Tape the tracing, face down, to a piece of foam. Then transfer the pencil graphite to the foam using a bone folder or other tool.

3. **Check.** Remove the tracing, making sure the graphite transferred.

4. **Cut out.** Cut out the pattern using scissors or a craft knife

5. **Mount.** Make an acrylic glass stamp base to fit the design. Peel off the paper backing from the foam and stick the pieces onto the glass. Use the pattern under the glass as a guide if needed.

6. **Mix paint.** Mix the Teal paint with textile medium.

4

7. **Prep and test the stamp.** Prepare your workspace for stamping. Load your stamp with paint. On a scrap of fabric, test the stamp. Make any adjustments to the stamp that you see are needed.

8. **Protect the pillowcase.** Place parchment paper or cardboard inside the pillowcase to protect the backside of the pillowcase.

5

8

9

9. Start stamping. Load the stamp with paint again and begin stamping your pillowcase. Place the first stamp on the left side of the pillowcase about 3½" (8.9 cm) from the bottom seam of the pillowcase. Crop about ¾" (2 cm) of the left side of the stamp off, allowing it to hang off the edge of the pillowcase.

10. Continue stamping the row. When placing the next stamp, rotate the stamp 180 degrees so the scallop shape is facing downward. Align the flat side with the flat side of the first stamp, but shift the new stamp to the right as shown. Continue stamping the row, leaving about 1¼" (3.2 cm) between each stamp that is facing the same way. Repeat this process for a second row above the first (shown in the step 12 photo).

10

11. Prepare to draw lines. Mix the black paint with textile medium.

12. Paint lines. Using a small paintbrush, paint two black lines above and below the pattern. I wanted a wonky, whimsical look for this pillow, so I freehanded the lines. If that feels intimidating to you, use painter's tape to guide you; in each side

seam, measure 1½" (3.8 cm) from the bottom of pillowcase, mark the seam with a water-soluble marker, and lay tape so the top of the tape meets the marks on both sides. Then paint a line at the top of the tape. When the paint is dry, lower the tape ½" (1.3 cm) down and paint your second line. Repeat for the top of the pillowcase.

PATTERN VARIATION IDEAS

BOTANICAL T-SHIRT

This is one of the few projects in the book that you can take out of the house to show off! And who wouldn't want to proudly wear their work? The design is completely color-customizable but is applied in a single application, so there are no worries about alignment. A mini hole punch is the trick to getting the neat, tiny circles in the center of the flower.

TOOLS & MATERIALS

▹ Prewashed white cotton T-shirt
▹ Botanical stamp pattern (page 160)

STAMPMAKING SUPPLIES

▹ Pencil
▹ Tracing paper
▹ Double-sided tape
▹ Craft foam with adhesive backing
▹ Bone folder paper creaser (optional)
▹ Scissors
▹ Craft knife
▹ Cutting mat
▹ 8½" x 11" (22 x 28 cm) sheet of acrylic glass
▹ Permanent marker
▹ Ruler/straightedge
▹ Safety glasses

PAINTING SUPPLIES

▹ Acrylic craft paint in 3 colors: Coral Cove, Yellow Ochre, Raw Sienna
▹ Textile medium
▹ Paint palette
▹ Craft foam brushes
▹ ⅛" (0.3 cm) hole punch or ¼" (0.6 cm) (standard-sized) hole punch
▹ Craft paper/fabric/plastic
▹ Wet wipes or wet paper towels
▹ Baren (optional)
▹ Cardboard
▹ Small paintbrush (optional)

1. **Trace.** Tape a piece of tracing paper to the pattern provided. Use a pencil to trace the pattern.

2. **Transfer.** Tape the tracing, face down, to a piece of foam. Then transfer the pencil graphite to the foam using a bone folder or other tool.

3. **Check.** Remove the tracing, making sure the graphite transferred.

4. **Cut out.** Cut out the flower using a craft knife and/or scissors.

5. **Punch dots.** Use a ⅛" (0.3 cm) hole punch to punch out dots in the flower center. If you have a standard-sized hole punch, which is larger, that will work too—just ignore the pattern and punch 3 to 5 holes instead.

6. **Mount.** Make an acrylic glass stamp base to fit the flower—you should be able to use an entire sheet. Peel off the paper backing from the foam and stick the flower onto the glass. Use the pattern under the glass as a guide if needed. Use the edge of a craft knife or a pair of tweezers to help place tiny pieces.

7. **Mix paint.** Mix all three paint colors with textile medium.

8. **Prep and test the stamp.** Prepare your workspace for stamping. Load your stamp with paint. Because this stamp is so large, you will need to work quickly while loading your stamp with paint so everything stays wet. On a scrap of fabric, test the stamp. Make any adjustments to the stamp that you see are needed.

4

5

9. Start stamping. Find the center of the T-shirt by folding it in half lengthwise, then creasing the fabric with your hand. Place a piece of cardboard inside the shirt to protect the backside of the shirt. Working quickly, load your stamp with paint and carefully place the stamp in the center of the shirt.

You'll only get one shot at it! Because it's a large stamp, I recommend using a baren or other tool to press it down and ensure good contact.

10. Touch up. Finish by using a small paintbrush to touch up any areas that need a bit more paint.

Any stamp can become a T-shirt! Here are two examples using block-printing stamps: the Woodland Mushroom stamp (pattern on page 162) and the Take Flight stamp (pattern on page 157). And see another stamp in action on page 24. Play with placement and color to suit your shirt and personal style.

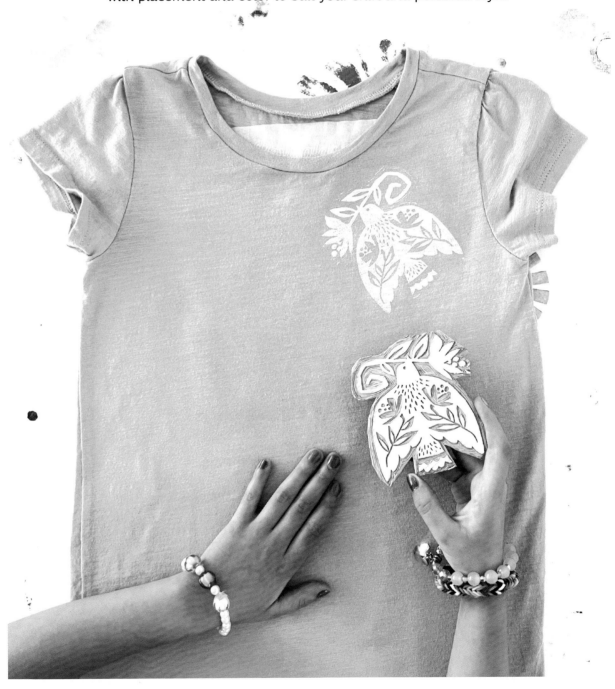

PATTERN VARIATION IDEAS

GEOMETRIC WRAPPING FABRIC

It's up to you whether you give this wrapping fabric away with the gift or take it back to use again another day! In this project, you'll use your skills to carefully align and build a design that covers a large area. You'll also learn some cool extras: how to make different kinds of ribbon to tie your gift closed.

TOOLS & MATERIALS

- 28" x 28" (71.1 x 71.1 cm) premade, prewashed white cotton tea towel
- Geometric stamp pattern (page 158)

STAMPMAKING SUPPLIES

- Pencil
- Tracing paper
- Double-sided tape
- Craft foam with adhesive backing
- Bone folder paper creaser (optional)
- Scissors
- Craft knife
- Cutting mat
- 8 ½" x 11" (22 x 28 cm) sheet of acrylic glass, or scraps of sufficient size (refer to pattern)
- Permanent marker
- Ruler/straightedge
- Safety glasses

PAINTING SUPPLIES

- Acrylic craft paint in 4 colors: Windsor Blue, New Leaf Green, Christmas Red, Sea Glass
- Textile medium
- Paint palette
- Craft foam brush
- Craft paper/fabric/plastic
- Wet wipes or wet paper towels
- Baren (optional)
- Small paintbrush (optional)

Don't miss the bonus stamped ribbon ideas on pages 102–103!

1. **Trace.** Tape a piece of tracing paper to the pattern provided. Use a pencil to trace the pattern.

2. **Transfer.** Tape the tracing, face down, to a piece of foam. Then transfer the pencil graphite to the foam using a bone folder or other tool.

3. **Check.** Remove the tracing, making sure the graphite transferred.

4. **Cut out.** Cut out the design using a craft knife, a ruler (or other straightedge to act as a guide), and scissors.

5. **Mount.** Make two acrylic glass stamp bases to fit the two designs—one for the circle and one for the block shapes. Peel off the paper backing from the foam and stick the designs onto the glass. Use the pattern under the glass as a guide if needed. For this design, the block shapes need to be quite precisely placed so that they align when stamped in sets of four.

6. **Mix paint.** Mix the blue paint with textile medium.

7. **Prep and test the stamp.** Prepare your workspace for stamping. Load your stamp with paint. On a scrap of fabric, test the stamp. Rotate the stamp at a 45-degree angle for each placement, creating a diamond shape. Make any adjustments to the stamp that you see are needed, and practice until you feel confident making the diamond shape.

8. **Start stamping.** When you are ready, start stamping on the tea towel, beginning in the bottom right corner. It's easy for the squares to fail to line up properly. Correct this, as best you can, by pulling the fabric slightly to make the stamps line up or simply allowing the stamps to overlap slightly to compensate. Keep in mind that imperfections add interest! Continue stamping the entire tea towel. Allow the paint to dry before continuing.

9. Test the next stamp and color. Mix textile medium with the other three paint colors. Using one of the colors, test the circle stamp on the same scrap fabric used before and make any adjustments needed.

10. Stamp the second design. Notice how, in the spot where four of the diamond shapes meet, an "X" is formed. Stamp circles on top of each "X" in a single vertical row. Starting from the bottom "X" again, move your stamp over to the left, skipping the next two "X" intersections, and stamp red circles in the third "X" intersection, all the way up the column. Then, stamp red circles centered between the two existing columns but shifted one "row" up. This will create staggered columns of the color with columns reserved for the other two colors.

11. Continue stamping circles. Repeat this process with the green and then the yellow paint colors, making sure each color is staggered.

PATTERN VARIATION IDEAS

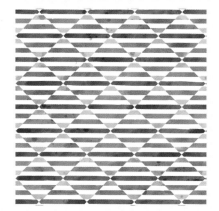

BONUS! BURST RIBBON

You'll need the standard supplies used in the main project, plus 1½" (3.8 cm) light blue cotton ribbon. I used the same blue acrylic craft paint shade as in the main project.

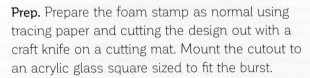

Prep. Prepare the foam stamp as normal using tracing paper and cutting the design out with a craft knife on a cutting mat. Mount the cutout to an acrylic glass square sized to fit the burst.

Stamp! Mix your paint with textile medium and prepare your workspace. If you are stamping several yards of ribbon at once, consider how you can extend your work surface to allow your paint to dry. Maybe drape the freshly stamped ribbon over an ironing board or a chair covered in an old towel. When you're ready, load your stamp with paint and test it on the end of the ribbon. Make adjustments to the stamp as desired, then get stamping!

BONUS! CONFETTI RIBBON

You'll need the standard supplies used in the main project, plus ½" (1.3 cm) white twill tape and a ¼" (0.6 cm) sponge dauber. I used all the same acrylic craft paint shades as in the main project.

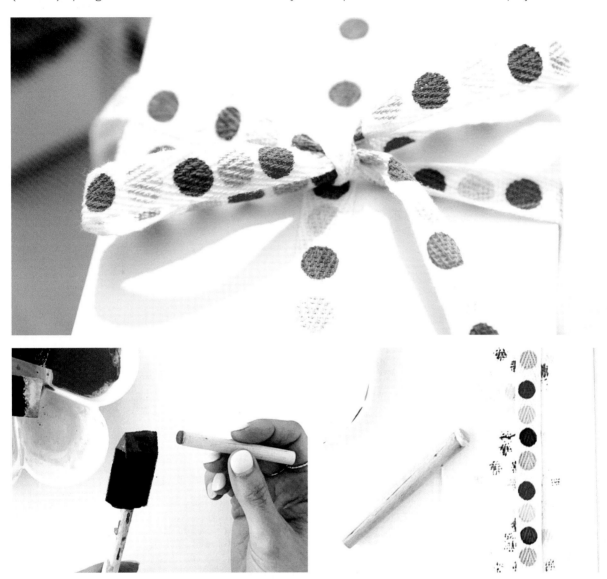

Prep. Prepare your workspace for stamping. If you will be stamping several yards of ribbon at once, consider how you can extend your work surface to allow your paint to dry. Maybe drape the freshly stamped ribbon over an ironing board or a chair covered in an old towel. Mix all four paint colors with textile medium. Use a foam brush to load your dauber with blue paint.

Stamp! On one end of the ribbon, begin stamping. Reapply paint to the dauber every third stamp or so. Place a ruler next to the ribbon to help guide your spacing. Leave about a 1¼" (3.2 cm) gap in between each blue dot, carefully shifting the ribbon as you go. When you're done with that color, clean the dauber with water and dab out the excess water. Repeat with yellow, red, and, finally, green paint.

CHAPTER 4:
Block-Printing Projects

Are you ready for some block printing? This chapter features a selection of satisfyingly complex block-printing stamps and ways to use them. Enjoy the meditative experience of carving the blocks and the satisfying experience of seeing your creations come to life in ink. You're sure to use these sturdy stamps again and again.

If needed, refer to the foundational block-printing tutorial on pages 38–47 for more technical guidance on executing the project steps.

BRIGHT PALMS PILLOWCASE

This deceptively simple stamp pattern holds a lot of potential for variation. While making this pillowcase, you'll learn how to incorporate acrylic paint as an additional feature alongside your ink-printed design, plus use a sponge dauber for easy circles.

TOOLS & MATERIALS

- 20" x 20" (50.8 x 50.8 cm) premade, prewashed white cotton pillowcase
- Bright Palms stamp pattern (page 166)

STAMPMAKING SUPPLIES

- Pencil
- Tracing paper
- Double-sided tape
- 4" x 6" (10 x 15.2 cm) rubber carving block
- Bone folder paper creaser (optional)
- Scissors, or craft knife and cutting mat
- Carving tools
- Permanent marker
- Craft paper/fabric/plastic

PAINTING SUPPLIES

- Fabric ink in 3 colors: green, white, blue
- Paper plate or paint palette
- Palette knife
- 8" x 10" (20.3 x 25.4 cm) sheet of acrylic glass, baking sheet, or other flat surface
- Soft-rubber brayer
- Wet wipes or wet paper towels
- Baren (optional)
- Cardboard
- Small paintbrush
- Acrylic paint in 2 colors: Hunter Green, New Leaf Green
- Textile medium
- ¼" (0.6 cm) sponge dauber
- Foam brush

1. **Trace.** Tape a piece of tracing paper to the pattern provided. Use a pencil to trace the pattern. There is no need to trace the dots—they will not be part of the final block stamp.

2. **Transfer.** Tape the tracing, face down, to the rubber carving block. Then transfer the pencil graphite to the block using a bone folder or other tool.

3. **Check.** Remove the tracing, making sure the graphite transferred.

4. **Cut out.** You can skip the coloring step for this simple design. Instead, go straight to cutting out and carving. Use a craft knife to cut away the excess block around the outside of the design, making a neat circle.

5. **Carve.** Carve the design, removing the design itself and switching between different carving blades as needed.

6. **Make a reference mark.** Mark the top of the stamp on the backside with a permanent marker. This will help with placement, since the design is completely round and you can't see how it is oriented once you flip it over.

7. **Prep and mix.** Prepare your workspace, then mix your ink color on a paper plate or paint palette. For this project, I wanted a bright teal color. Begin by mixing 4 parts white, 2 parts blue, and 1 part green. The color-mixing process can include some trial and error. Continue adding small amounts of different inks until you are satisfied with the color.

8. **Make the ink well.** Add a few tablespoons of ink to your acrylic glass sheet or other flat surface. Use a brayer to pull the ink down vertically, then horizontally. Repeat until you have a nice, even coat of ink on the brayer.

5

6

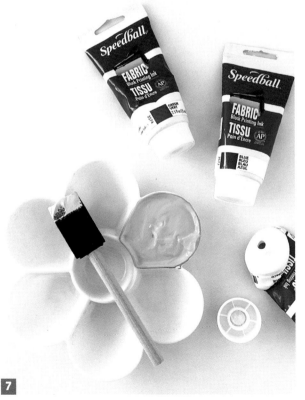

7

8

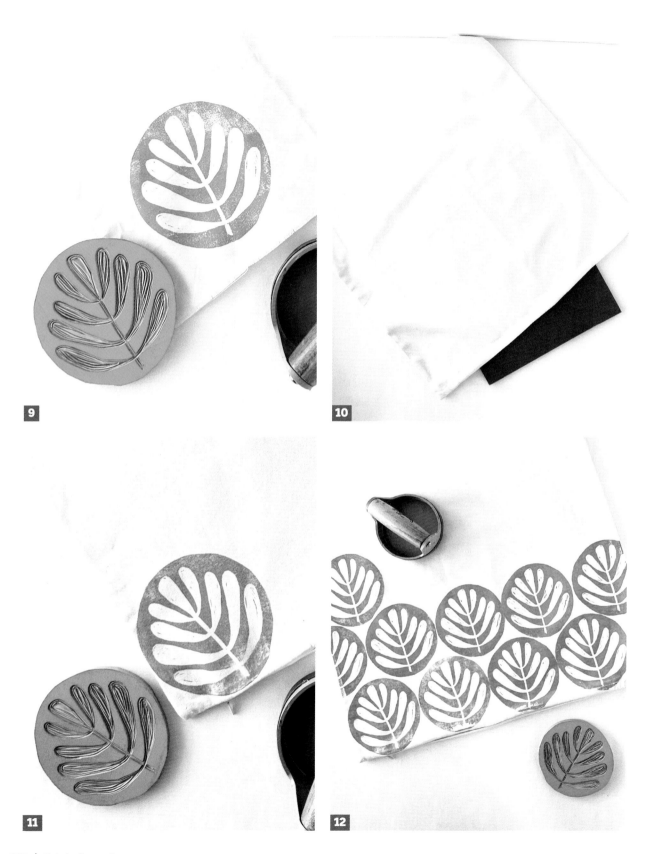

9. Test the stamp. Clean your hands, roll an even coat of ink onto the stamp block, and test the stamp on a scrap of fabric. Make any adjustments to the stamp that you see are needed.

10. Prep the pillowcase. Add a piece of cardboard to the inside of the pillowcase to protect the backside.

11. Start stamping. Load the stamp with ink. Begin printing by placing the block in the bottom corner, cropping off just a tiny bit of the left edge of the stamp. Press down with even pressure.

12. Keep stamping. Continue stamping along the bottom of the pillowcase, just barely touching the previous print. When you begin the next row above the first, align the stamp in between the two prints below to create a staggered effect. Stamp the whole pillowcase this way.

13. Touch up. If you want to do any touch-ups to the design, while the ink is still wet, use a small paintbrush and a dabbing motion to lightly fill in any spots that didn't get enough ink.

14. Mix acrylic paint for dots. Mix the Hunter Green acrylic paint with textile medium.

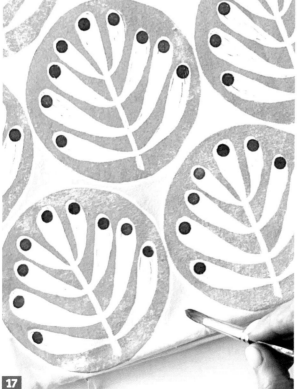

15. Add dots. Add little dots to the ends of each negative-space leaf by applying paint to the ¼" (0.6 cm) sponge dauber with a foam brush, then stamping. Reapply the paint to the sponge dauber every third stamp or so. Dot every leaf in the pattern this way.

16. Mix acrylic paint for the background. Mix the New Leaf Green acrylic paint with textile medium.

17. Paint the background. Paint around the outside of each palm stamp, leaving just a tiny outline of white around each stamp. Color in the entire background this way.

Try applying this pattern to a fabric clutch! This clutch is made using the same technique as the Bright Palms Pillowcase project, just with some extra hand painting.

PATTERN VARIATION IDEAS

FANNED LEAF TABLE RUNNER

One of the largest projects in the book, this table runner is sure to catch the eye of guests. It's difficult to mix the same exact color twice, so, because this is such a big endeavor, you'll need to prepare (and potentially store) a lot of ink for the execution.

TOOLS & MATERIALS

▶ 14" x 72" (35.6 x 183 cm) premade, prewashed white cotton table runner
▶ Fanned Leaf stamp pattern (page 155)

STAMPMAKING SUPPLIES

▶ Pencil
▶ Tracing paper
▶ Double-sided tape
▶ 4" x 6" (10 x 15.2 cm) rubber carving block
▶ Bone folder paper creaser (optional)
▶ Permanent marker
▶ Carving tools
▶ Scissors, or craft knife and cutting mat
▶ Rubbing alcohol
▶ Paper towel
▶ Craft paper/fabric/plastic

PAINTING SUPPLIES

▶ Fabric ink in 3 colors: red, white, yellow
▶ Palette knife
▶ Sealable storage container (such as a plastic tub or glass jar)
▶ 8" x 10" (20.3 x 25.4 cm) sheet of acrylic glass, baking sheet, or other flat surface
▶ Soft-rubber brayer
▶ Wet wipes or wet paper towels
▶ Baren (optional)
▶ Small paintbrush (optional)

1. **Trace.** Tape a piece of tracing paper to the pattern provided. Use a pencil to trace the pattern.

2. **Transfer.** Tape the tracing, face down, to the rubber carving block. Then transfer the pencil graphite to the block using a bone folder or other tool.

3. **Check.** Remove the tracing, making sure the graphite transferred.

4. **Color in.** Color in the negative space (the areas that will be cut away) using a black permanent marker. Then color in an outline around the whole design.

5. **Carve.** Carve the design, removing all the colored areas and switching between different carving blades as needed.

6. **Cut out and clean up.** After you've carved the entire design, cut away the excess block around the outside of the design. Then use rubbing alcohol on a paper towel to remove any excess marker ink from the stamp.

7. **Prep and mix.** Prepare your workspace, then mix your ink color in a resealable container—because this project is more time consuming, you might not be able to finish in one setting, so you want to keep the ink fresh. You will need to mix about 8 ounces (28 grams) of ink total; it is very difficult to mix the color again and have it match exactly. For this project, I wanted a bright coral color. Begin by mixing 4 parts red, 2 parts white, and 1 part yellow. Continue adding small amounts of different inks until you are satisfied with the color.

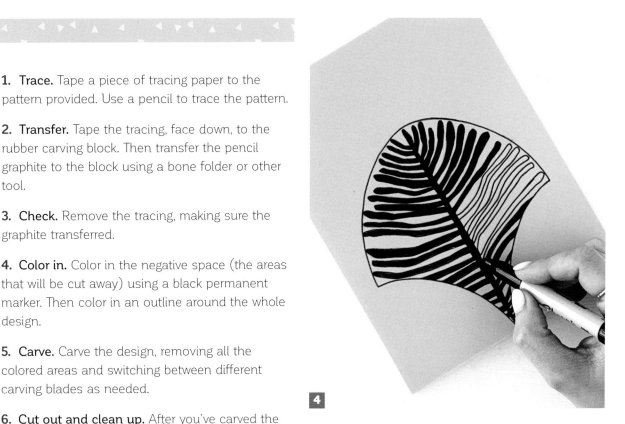

4

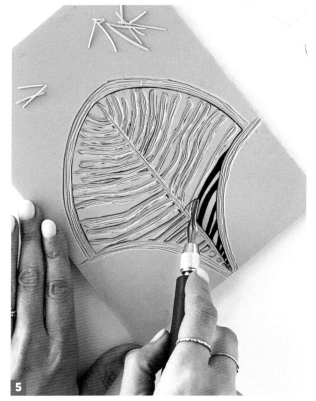

5

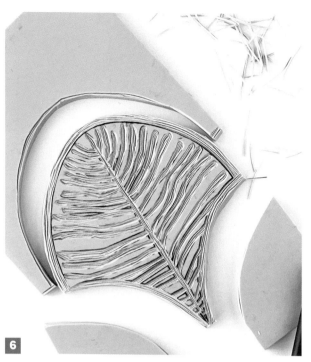

6

7

8

9

8. Make the ink well. Add a few tablespoons of ink to your acrylic glass sheet or other flat surface. Use a brayer to pull the ink down vertically, then horizontally. Repeat until you have a nice, even coat of ink on the brayer.

9. Test the stamp. Clean your hands, roll an even coat of ink onto the stamp block, and test the stamp on a scrap of fabric. Make any adjustments to the stamp that you see are needed.

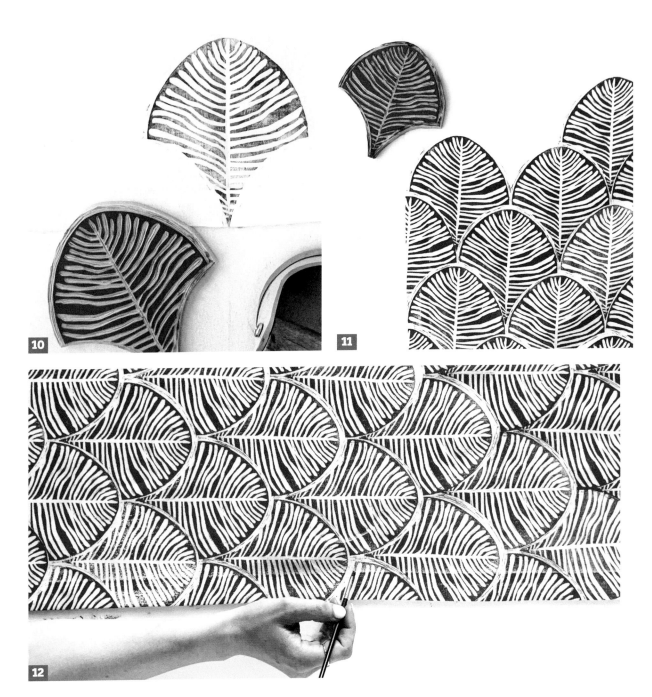

10. Start stamping. When the stamp is ready, load the stamp with ink. Find the center of your table runner by folding it in half lengthwise, meeting corners to corners, then creasing the fabric with your hand. Begin printing by centering the block on the crease line. Press down with even pressure.

11. Finish stamping. Repeat this process, lining up each stamp with the previous print as you go. The shape of the leaf will create a seamless fill all the way up and across the table runner.

12. Touch up. If you want to do any touch-ups to the design, while the ink is still wet, use a small paintbrush and a dabbing motion to lightly fill in any spots that didn't get enough ink.

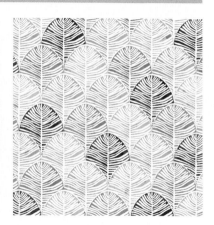

METAMORPHOSIS TOTE

Here is another show-off-able project! This canvas tote layers two delightfully complex moth stamps in two colors. The ink brand I used is not officially recommended for use on canvas. I can understand why, because it doesn't absorb into the canvas the way it does to other fabrics, and the stamped design didn't look quite as crisp initially. But I used a lot of ink and touched up the image with a paintbrush, and I'm really happy with the result. Take this as a lesson—you can make unexpected things work!

TOOLS & MATERIALS

▸ Premade, prewashed purple cotton tote
▸ Metamorphosis stamp pattern (page 166)

STAMPMAKING SUPPLIES

▸ Pencil
▸ Tracing paper
▸ Double-sided tape
▸ 5" x 7" (12.7 x 17.8 cm) soft linoleum carving block or 4" x 6" (10 x 15.2 cm) rubber carving block
▸ Bone folder paper creaser (optional)
▸ Permanent marker
▸ Carving tools
▸ Scissors, or craft knife and cutting mat
▸ Rubbing alcohol
▸ Paper towel
▸ Craft paper/fabric/plastic

PAINTING SUPPLIES

▸ Fabric ink in 3 colors: red, white, blue
▸ Paper plate or paint palette
▸ Palette knife
▸ Foam brush
▸ 8" x 10" (20.3 x 25.4 cm) sheet of acrylic glass, baking sheet, or other flat surface
▸ Soft-rubber brayer
▸ Wet wipes or wet paper towels
▸ Baren (optional)
▸ Small paintbrush (optional)

1. **Trace.** Tape a piece of tracing paper to the pattern provided. Use a pencil to trace the pattern.

2. **Transfer.** Tape the tracing, face down, to the carving block. Then transfer the pencil graphite to the block using a bone folder or other tool.

3. **Check.** Remove the tracing, making sure the graphite transferred.

4. **Color in.** Color in the negative space (the areas that will be cut away) using a black permanent marker, including an outline around each moth.

5. **Cut out.** Cut away the excess block around the outside of each moth. Include a border about ¼" to ½" (0.6 to 1.3 cm) wide around each moth (more than the black outline). If you're new to carving, I recommend doing this step after carving instead—that way, there is a little more block to hold on to while carving.

6. **Carve the first moth.** Carve the first moth design, removing all the colored areas and switching between different carving blades as needed. Carve all the way to the edge of the stamp all the way around.

7. **Finish carving and clean up.** Repeat this process with the second moth. After you've carved both moths, use rubbing alcohol on a paper towel to remove any excess marker ink from the stamps.

4

5

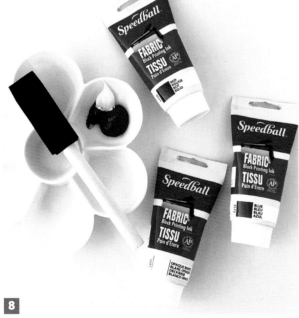

8. Prep and mix. Prepare your workspace, then mix your ink colors on a paper plate or paint palette. For this project, for one moth, I wanted a reddish-purple color to go with my tote bag. Begin by mixing 3 parts red, 2 parts white, and 1 part blue. Continue adding small amounts of different inks until you are satisfied with the color.

9. Make the ink well. Add a few tablespoons of ink to your acrylic glass sheet or other flat surface. Use a brayer to pull the ink down vertically, then horizontally. Repeat until you have a nice, even coat of ink on the brayer.

10

11

12

10. Test the first stamp. Clean your hands, roll an even coat of ink onto the first stamp block, and test the stamp on a scrap of fabric. Make any adjustments to the stamp that you see are needed.

11. Stamp the purple moth. Insert cardboard into the tote bag to protect the backside. Load the stamp with ink and make the first print. Continue printing with this moth, turning and tilting the stamp slightly each time you place it. Remember that you will be adding the other moth stamp later, so allow room for that. Don't forget to do some stamping on the straps too!

12. Touch up. If you want to do any touch-ups to the prints, while the ink is still wet, use a small paintbrush and a dabbing motion to lightly fill in any spots that didn't get enough ink.

13. Stamp the white moth. Repeat this process with the second moth stamp and white ink: test it first, then stamp it where desired.

14. Stamp the other side. If you want both sides of your tote to be stamped, wait for the first side to dry completely before flipping the tote over and repeating the whole stamping process.

PATTERN VARIATION IDEAS

TAKE FLIGHT COASTERS

Some block-printing stamps have a lot of complexity and precision built into the design, and you want your hard work to go far. How about on a full set of coasters? You could make a matching set like I did, all in one color, or a rainbow set, or a set that coordinates with your living room.

TOOLS & MATERIALS

- 4½" x 4½" (11.4 x 11.4 cm) premade, prewashed white coasters
- Take Flight stamp pattern (page 157)

STAMPMAKING SUPPLIES

- Pencil
- Tracing paper
- Double-sided tape
- 4" x 6" (10 x 15.2 cm) rubber carving block
- Bone folder paper creaser (optional)
- Permanent marker
- Carving tools
- Scissors, or craft knife and cutting mat
- Rubbing alcohol
- Paper towel
- Craft paper/fabric/plastic

PAINTING SUPPLIES

- Fabric ink in 1 color: black
- 8" x 10" (20.3 x 25.4 cm) sheet of acrylic glass, baking sheet, or other flat surface
- Soft-rubber brayer
- Wet wipes or wet paper towels
- Baren (optional)
- Small paintbrush (optional)

What a great project to make as a housewarming gift for a friend or loved one!

1. **Trace.** Tape a piece of tracing paper to the pattern provided. Use a pencil to trace the pattern.

2. **Transfer.** Tape the tracing, face down, to the rubber carving block. Then transfer the pencil graphite to the block using a bone folder or other tool.

3. **Check.** Remove the tracing, making sure the graphite transferred.

4. **Color in.** Color in the negative space (the areas that will be cut away) using a black permanent marker. Then color in an outline, about ¼" (0.6 cm) wide, around the whole design.

5. **Carve.** Carve the design, removing all the colored areas and switching between different carving blades as needed. Make sure to carve away the outline too.

6. **Cut out and clean up.** After you've carved the entire design, cut away the excess block around the outside of the design. Then use rubbing alcohol on a paper towel to remove any excess marker ink from the stamp.

7. **Prep.** Prepare your workspace. There is no need to mix colors in a palette because we are using pure black. Simply add about a tablespoon of ink to your acrylic glass sheet or other flat surface.

8. **Make the ink well.** Use a brayer to pull the ink down vertically, then horizontally. Repeat until you have a nice, even coat of ink on the brayer.

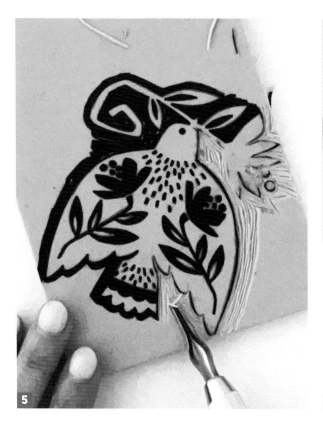

9

10

9. Test the stamp. Clean your hands, roll an even coat of ink onto the stamp block, and test the stamp on a scrap of fabric. Make any adjustments to the stamp that you see are needed

10. Stamp. When the stamp is ready, load the stamp with ink. Place the stamp in the center of the coaster and print by applying even pressure. Repeat for each coaster.

11. Touch up. If you want to do any touch-ups to the prints, while the ink is still wet, use a small paintbrush and a dabbing motion to lightly fill in any spots that didn't get enough ink.

The technique for making a journal like this one is identical to the technique for the Take Flight Coasters project—the only difference is the media being stamped on! Take extra care with your stamp carving and application, since the surface of a journal is hard and inflexible. Find this bonus block-printing stamp pattern on page 159.

PATTERN VARIATION IDEAS

CHAPTER 5:
Next-Level Projects

This chapter features projects that incorporate special new techniques, unique tools, or extra complexity. You'll learn to make a stamp from a potato, combine a plethora of different stamps into a cohesive design, mask negative space with tape, and design a beautiful batik using paint washes. Let your creativity loose!

If needed, refer to the foundational foam-stamping and block-printing tutorials on pages 28–37 and 38–47 for more technical guidance on executing the project steps.

LUNA TEA TOWEL

Stamps can be made from just about anything, from the end of a toilet paper roll to a bunch of rubber bands wrapped around a block. One of my favorite techniques is stamping with natural items. With the textures and shapes of fruits, veggies, and leaves, you can create beautiful patterns with an organic vibe. This potato technique is one of the simplest and quickest ways to create a stamp!

TOOLS & MATERIALS

- 18" x 28" (45.7 x 71.1 cm) premade, prewashed white cotton tea towel
- 1 or more small potatoes

STAMPMAKING SUPPLIES

- Knife and cutting board
- Spare tea towel or paper towels

I bet you didn't open this book and expect to be making stamps out of potatoes. Well, I'm here to tell you it's a blast!

PAINTING SUPPLIES

- Acrylic craft paint in 3 colors: Violet, Raw Sienna, Sea Glass
- Textile medium
- Paint palette
- Craft foam brushes
- Forks
- Craft paper/fabric/plastic
- Wet wipes or wet paper towels

1. **Cut into halves.** Cut a potato in half widthwise.

2. **Cut into quarters.** Cut each piece again lengthwise so you have four quarter-potatoes.

3. **Remove excess moisture.** Dab the cut surfaces of the potatoes on a piece of cloth or paper towel to absorb as much of the moisture as possible.

4. **Mix paint.** Mix all three paint colors with textile medium.

5. **Prep the stamp.** Prepare your workspace for stamping. Use a foam brush to add paint to one cut side of the first potato.

6. **Test the stamp.** On a scrap of fabric, text the first potato stamp. Add paint to the other potatoes to test their stamp shapes as well.

7. **Figure out a design.** Try out different patterns, colors, and potatoes to decide on a combo you like best.

8. **Stamp.** Once you've decided on a pattern, prepare your workspace. Then begin stamping your tea towel. If you find the potatoes are small and difficult to hold on to, use forks as handles. Reapply paint each time you stamp.

9. **Finish.** Continue stamping until you're finished with your design. Go slowly and really think about which color and direction to stamp—it's easy to go too fast and make a mistake!

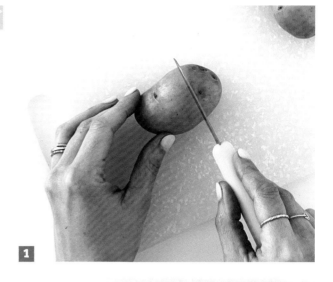

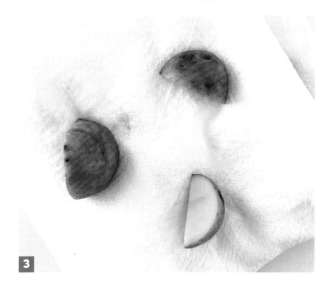

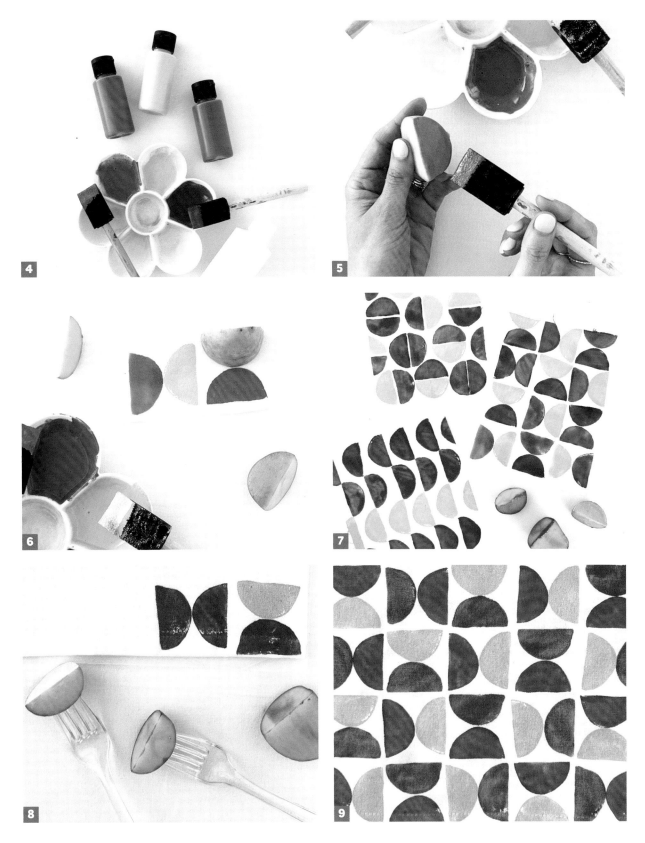

WALLFLOWER HANGING

You've already seen a few projects in this book that combine different techniques in small ways. Layering your ideas and blending different methods gives you endless possibilities for your fabric projects. Here is a multi-technique, multi-stamp project that shows you how to make a truly custom item. I hope it inspires you, gets your creative juices flowing, and helps build your confidence for creating your own unique pieces!

TOOLS & MATERIALS

- 12" (30.5 cm) magnetic poster frames
- Canvas fabric
- Stamp patterns: Bold Blossom (page 164), Botanical (page 160), Cheerful Blooms (page 163), Colorful Cosmo (page 155), Burst Ribbon (page 156)

STAMPMAKING SUPPLIES

- Pencil
- Tracing paper
- Double-sided tape
- Craft foam with adhesive backing
- Bone folder paper creaser (optional)
- Scissors
- Craft knife
- Cutting mat
- 8½" x 11" (22 x 28 cm) sheets of acrylic glass (as many as needed to make the stamps)
- Permanent marker
- Ruler/straightedge
- Safety glasses
- Water-soluble marker
- Ruler

PAINTING SUPPLIES

- Painter's tape
- Acrylic craft paint in 3 colors: Warm Bisque, Raw Sienna, Terra Cotta
- Textile medium
- Paint palette
- Craft foam brushes
- Craft paper/fabric/plastic
- Small paintbrush
- Wet wipes or wet paper towels
- Baren (optional)
- ¼" (0.6 cm) sponge dauber
- ½" (1.3 cm) sponge dauber
- Fusible fabric tape
- Iron and ironing board

1. **Make all the stamps.** Make any of the listed stamps that you haven't already made.

2. **Draw out the canvas.** Make sure your top right canvas corner is squared. Lay the top and the bottom of your magnetic frame about 16" (40.5 cm) apart, 1" (2.5 cm) vertically and horizontally from the top right corner of your canvas (counting the width of the frame as the inch from the top). Using a ruler, draw lines from the outside edges of the top frame down to the outside edges of the bottom frame on each side—this delineates the edges of the "live," to-be-stamped area of the project. Next, draw an additional vertical line 1" (2.5 cm) from and parallel to the left edge line, then draw a final horizontal line from the bottom of the last line all along the bottom edge of the bottom frame piece to the far raw edge of the canvas.

3. **Cut the canvas.** Cut the rectangle of canvas out along the far left and bottom cut lines (the last lines you drew). You now have a canvas area to paint with sufficient "seam allowance" for finishing it neatly at the end. You can put away the frame pieces for now.

4. **Mask the vase.** Fold the canvas in half, meeting corners to corners, then crease with your hand. On the crease line, starting from the bottom of the live area, create a wonky, vaselike shape by outlining it with little pieces of painter's tape.

5. **Paint the vase.** Mix the Raw Sienna paint with textile medium. Using a small paintbrush, make horizontal lines inside the vase. You can freehand these or use painter's tape to help guide you.

6. **Prep the first stamp.** Mix the Warm Bisque paint with textile medium. Load paint onto the flower part of the Botanical stamp only. Do not put paint on the stem.

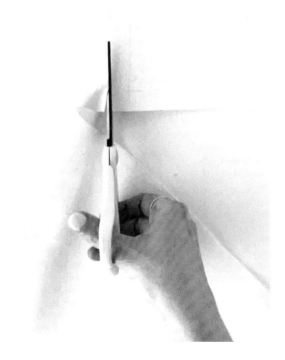

7. Add the main flower. Stamp the flower above the top right side of the vase at a slight angle.

8. Add more flowers. Continuing with the same color, start adding other flower stamps, working outward from the initial Botanical stamp. Use the larger stamps first, including Colorful Cosmo and pieces from Cheerful Blooms.

9

11

9. Add even more flowers. Continue adding more floral stamps. From the Bold Blossom stamps here, I only used petals #2 and #3 and the top (stamens) part of the stem.

10. Finish adding flowers. Continue filling in all the blank spaces with flower and leaf stamps, mainly from Bold Blossom and Cheerful Blooms. Work your way from larger to smaller stamps. Then, with a paintbrush, add a stem to the Botanical main flower, connecting it from the center of the flower to the top of the vase. (See the completed effect in the step 11 photo.)

11. Change colors. Mix the Terra Cotta paint with textile medium. Then stamp the center of some or all the flowers using the ring stamp from Cheerful Blooms and a sponge dauber. Apply paint to the sponge dauber with a craft foam brush and reapply the paint to the dauber every third stamp or so.

12

13

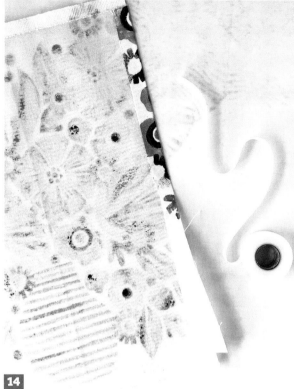

14

12. Add final flowers and dots. Add a few Terra Cotta flowers using the Burst Ribbon stamp. Then use more of your Warm Bisque paint mixture to dot the inside of these Burst Ribbon flowers.

13. Trim the corners. After everything has dried, cut out the four corners from the canvas.

14. "Hem" the edges. Fold all unfinished edges to the backside of the canvas and secure with fusible fabric tape, ironing to create the final bond. Here I am in the process of hemming the two sides and the bottom of the canvas, but in my case, the top edge was already finished, meaning it was not going to fray, so I did not have to fold or fuse it.

15. Assemble the wall hanging. Add the magnetic frames—these will pinch the canvas between them to securely hold the piece in place. You're done!

15

TAPE-MASKING TECHNIQUE

BAMBOO TEA TOWEL

Masking is the technique of covering certain areas of the fabric, then painting and/or stamping on top of them. The covered area will be protected from the paint and will have clean, precise edges. There are different ways to mask your fabric for different effects. In this project, we will freehand rip and place bits of painter's tape to create a cool bamboo forest effect.

TOOLS & MATERIALS

- 18" x 28" (45.7 x 71.1 cm) premade, prewashed white cotton tea towel

STAMPMAKING SUPPLIES

- 2" (5 cm)–wide painter's tape

It is honestly super meditative to sit and rip painter's tape to create this design. Peeling it up at the end is lots of fun too!

PAINTING SUPPLIES

- Acrylic craft paint in 1 color: Sea Glass
- Textile medium
- Paint palette
- Craft foam brush
- Craft paper/fabric/plastic
- Wet wipes or wet paper towels
- Baren (optional)

1. **Begin masking.** Start tearing off ½" to 1" (1.3 to 2.5 cm) pieces of tape. They do not need to be straight. As you go, stick them to the bottom edge of the towel. Leave about ½" to 1" (1.3 to 2.5 cm) of space between each piece of tape.

2. **Continue masking.** Each time you work on a new row above the previous row, align each piece of tape between the two pieces of tape below it to create a staggered effect where every area of white is completely bound by tape.

3. **Press down the tape.** Use a baren or your hand to press and smooth down all the corners and edges of all the tape.

4. **Mix paint.** Mix the Sea Glass paint with textile medium.

5. **Paint over the mask.** Use a foam brush to paint all the exposed parts of the tea towel. Be gentle so you don't accidentally peel up any of the pieces of tape with your brush.

6. **Reveal the design.** Allow the paint to fully dry. Then peel off the tape to reveal your design!

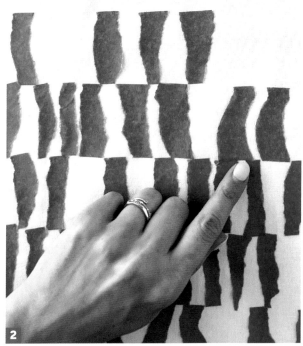

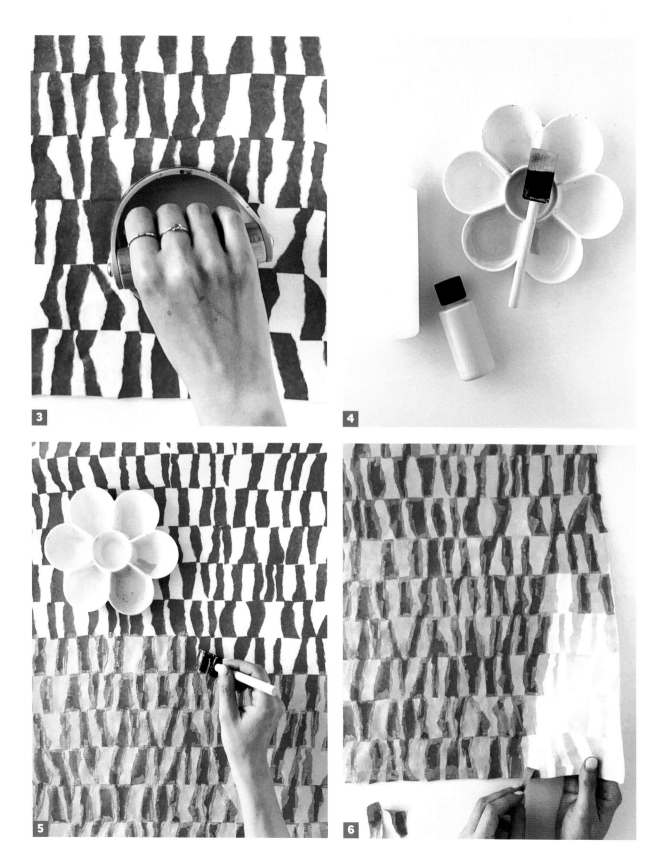

PRISM TEA TOWEL

You can use acrylic paint to create a soft, beautiful wash on fabric. This, plus foam stamping and a masking technique, allows you to achieve a stunning batik print effect. In this project, we'll also use one of the most ubiquitous craft supplies to create the mask: glue!

TOOLS & MATERIALS

- 18" x 28" (45.7 x 71.1 cm) premade, prewashed white cotton tea towel
- Scallop Shell stamp pattern (page 167)

STAMPMAKING SUPPLIES

- Water-soluble marker
- Pencil
- Tracing paper
- Double-sided tape
- Craft foam with adhesive backing
- Bone folder paper creaser (optional)
- Scissors
- Craft knife
- Cutting mat
- 8½" x 11" (22 x 28 cm) sheet of acrylic glass, or scraps of sufficient size (refer to pattern)
- Permanent marker
- Ruler/straightedge
- Safety glasses

PAINTING SUPPLIES

- Acrylic craft paint in 6 colors: Violet, Lavender, Sea Glass, Teal, Coral Cove, Yellow Ochre
- Textile medium
- Paint palette
- Craft foam brushes
- Craft paper/fabric/plastic
- Wet wipes or wet paper towels
- Baren (optional)
- Washable school glue
- 1" (2.5 cm) paintbrush

Who knew your average school glue could give such beautiful results?

1. **Draw wavy guidelines.** Using a water-soluble marker, draw three curvy, organic lines, at least 2" to 3" (5 to 7.6 cm) apart, across the tea towel.

2. **Mix paint.** Mix the Violet paint with textile medium.

3. **Make and prep the stamp.** Make a foam stamp using the Scallop Shell pattern (for more guidance, see page 30 or 88). Load the stamp with paint using a foam brush.

4. **Start stamping.** Begin stamping above and below the curvy lines you drew. Try to keep each print a consistent distance away from the lines themselves.

5. **Finish stamping.** Continue stamping until you've stamped all along both sides of all the lines. Make matched sets of "flowers" centered on the lines, instead of staggering the prints.

6. **Add glue masks.** Using washable school glue, add dash marks and lines to your piece to create masked areas. I added seed-shaped dollops in the large areas between the stamped sections and a few wavy lines on top of and along the soluble marker lines. Allow the glue to dry completely.

7. **Mix paint washes.** Mix each paint color with textile medium, then add in water and mix well to create paint washes. Test each color on a scrap of fabric to make sure each color is very watered down (practically the consistency of milk).

8. **Paint the fabric.** Using the watery colors and a 1" (2.5 cm) paintbrush, paint over the entire towel, switching to different colors as you go. Rinse your brush in between each color. You can paint right over the stamped areas if you don't want to be precise—the watery paint will only slightly alter the stamped colors, if at all.

9. **Wash to finish.** Wash and dry the towel in a washer and dryer—this will remove the glue neatly and cleanly with no need to peel it off by hand. Your final design will be revealed!

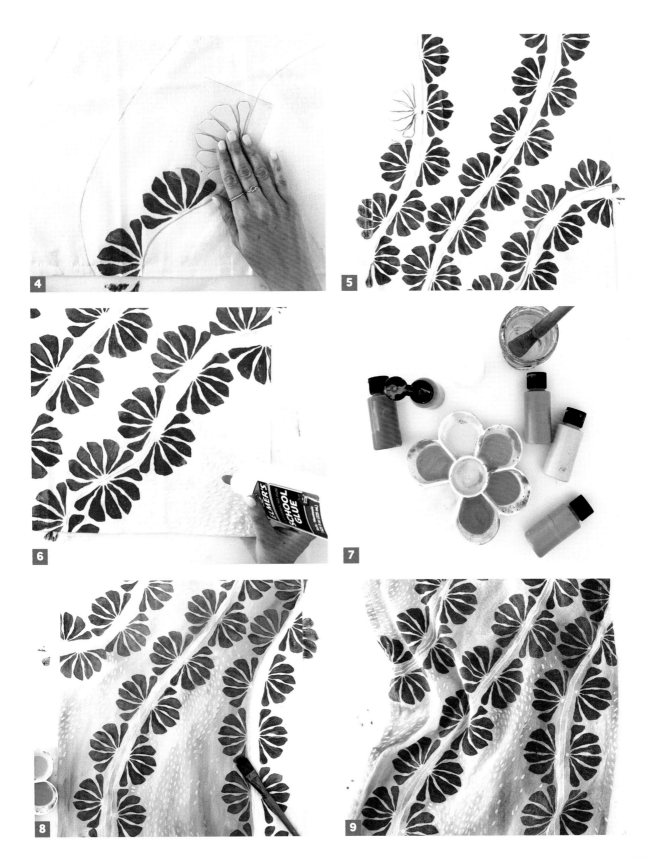

Finding Inspiration for Your Own Stamps

When looking to be inspired, it's so easy to hop on your phone and start scrolling. While the internet can be a wonderful resource, scrolling often leaves us feeling overwhelmed and discouraged. That's when we should remind ourselves to look up and pay attention to what's around us, not just what's on our tiny screens. By forcing ourselves to look at everyday items in different ways, we can begin to discover a unique perspective. Here are three projects inspired by everyday items.

Transforming items into art starts with observation. Instead of seeing them for the items they are, focus on the shapes, details, and colors. Next, allow your creativity to take over through sketching.

Experiment, play around, and try to envision the stamp your sketch could become. Is it intricate or simple? Then, begin to adjust your drawing, considering the stamp you want to create. For instance, when creating the Organic stamp, I fattened the stems and simplified the overall design. And for the Vintage Broach stamp, I added a border and a leaf embellishment in the corners. Adding your own unique touches keeps the design fresh. Once you've finalized your sketch, draw over it with a black marker, then begin making the stamp, experimenting and refining as you go! The possibilities are endless—just keep your eyes open and keep observing.

WROUGHT-IRON FENCE

I was inspired to take the shapes of this fence and bring them to vivid life in color! To re-create this design, use the Geometric Wrapping Paper pattern circle (page 158), which is 1¾" (4.5 cm) wide, and painter's tape for the rest of the design.

 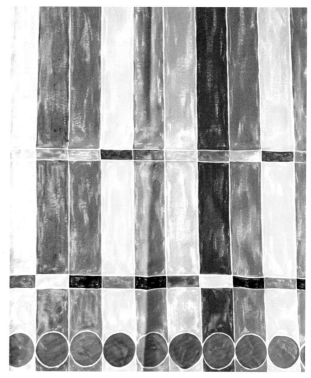

VINTAGE BROACH

I turned this gorgeous broach into a block-printing stamp that looks stunning on an otherwise unadorned hardcover journal. Grab the block-printing pattern on page 163!

ORGANIC BLOOMS

These gomphrena blooms, also known as globe amaranth, delighted me so much that I not only had to match my nail polish to them but also make a stamp of them! Find the foam-stamping pattern on page 156.

PATTERN APPENDIX

This appendix contains all the patterns shown in the book—including all the bonus ideas you've encountered within projects and on the Finding Inspiration pages. Each pattern page is perforated for removal from the book to make tracing the patterns fast and easy. Hold on to the removed pages in case you need the patterns again in the future. You can also download and print the patterns if needed by visiting www.betterdaybooks.com/fabric-stamping-patterns-download.

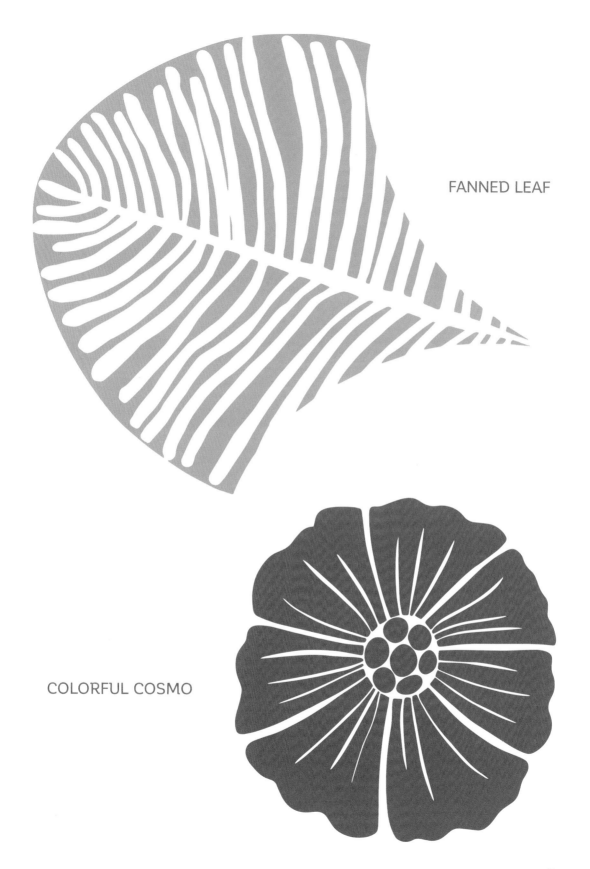

FANNED LEAF

COLORFUL COSMO

ORGANIC BLOOMS

BURST RIBBON

SUNBURST

Design is 2 separate stamps

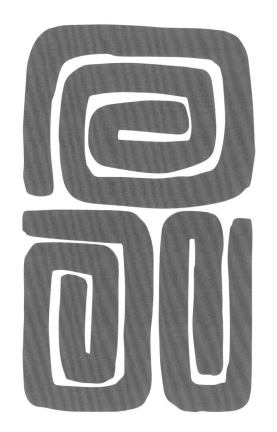

LABYRINTH

FOLKY SUNFLOWER

TAKE FLIGHT

GEOMETRIC

Design is 2 separate stamps

ARC

Design is 2 separate stamps

GARTER SNAKE

BOTANICAL

Design is 1 single stamp; tape the
halves together to use

GARDEN PARTY

WOODLAND MUSHROOM

VINTAGE BROACH

CHEERFUL BLOOMS

Design is 7 separate stamps; dauber paint dots are indicated in gray

BOLD BLOSSOM
Design is 6 separate stamps

Petals 1

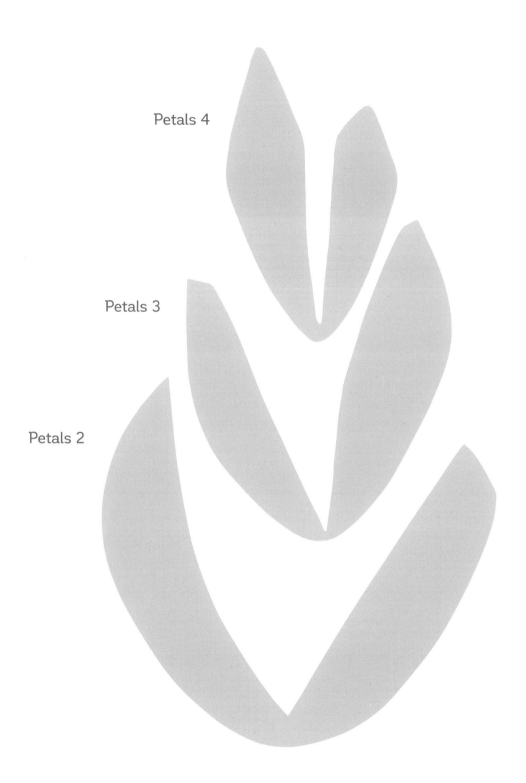

Petals 4

Petals 3

Petals 2

METAMORPHOSIS

Design is 2 separate stamps

BRIGHT PALMS

Dauber paint dots are
indicated in gray

SCALLOP SHELL

MOD FLOWER

Dauber paint dots are indicated in gray

INDEX

Note: Page numbers in *italics* indicate projects and patterns (in parentheses).

BETTER DAY BOOKS®

HAPPY · CREATIVE · CURATED

Business is personal at Better Day Books. We were founded on the belief that all people are creative and that making things by hand is inherently good for us. It's important to us that you know how much we appreciate your support. The book you are holding in your hands was crafted with the artistic passion of the author and brought to life by a team of wildly enthusiastic creatives who believed it could inspire you. If it did, please drop us a line and let us know about it. Connect with us on Instagram, post a photo of your art, and let us know what other creative pursuits you are interested in learning about. It all matters to us. You're kind of a big deal.

it's a good day to have a better day!

www.betterdaybooks.com

⊙ better_day_books